LUTHERAN
VOICES

Open the Doors
and See All the People
Stories of Congregational Identity
and Vocation

Norma Cook Everist

Augsburg Fortress

Minneapolis

To our children and our children's children, that they may be embraced
by communities of faith and in turn share God's love in the world.
I especially give thanks for Mark, Joel, Kirk, Rachel, Rebecca, Gwydion,
and Jennaya and for their many, diverse, creative ministries in daily life.

Large-quantity purchases or custom editions of this book are available at a discount from the publisher. For more information, contact the sales department at Augsburg Fortress, Publishers, P.O. Box 1209, Minneapolis, MN 55440-1209.

Direct Scripture quotations are from Revised Standard Version Bible, copyright © 1989 Division of Christian Education of the National Council of the Churches of Christ in the United States of America. Used by permission.

Library of Congress Cataloging-in-Publication Data
Everist, Norma Cook, 1938-
   Open the doors and see all the people : stories of congregational identity and vocation / Norma Cook Everist.
      p. cm.
   Includes bibliographical references.
   ISBN 0-8066-5161-X
1. Church. 2. Lutheran Church—Doctrines. 3. Church renewal—Lutheran Church.
4. Lutheran Church—United States. I. Title.
   BX8065.3.E84 2004
   284.1'35—dc22   2004023182

Editor: Susan R. Niemi

Cover Design: Koechel Peterson and Associates, Inc., Minneapolis, MN
                www.koechelpeterson.com

The paper used in this publication meets the minimum requirements of American National Standards for Information Sciences—Permanence of Paper for Printed Library Materials, ANSI Z329.48-1984. ♾ ™

Manufactured in the U.S.A.

09   08   07   06   05   1   2   3   4   5   6   7   8   9   10

Contents

Introduction

My sons tell me their mother is the only mother they know who takes notes at a parade—and most everywhere else she goes.

This is a journey book. I invite you, the reader, to go with me on my travels. I have visited dozens of congregations in their diverse communities over the past fifteen years, yes, taking notes. The book was written for your enjoyment; quite possibly it also will challenge you. Stories beget stories. Climb into the car with me, discover these congregations, and then look around and tell your own story of the place you live and worship and serve. The purpose of this book is to help congregations claim their identity in the body of Christ and be strengthened for their vocation in God's public world.

The congregations

The congregations described in this book were not carefully selected to be examples of ministry for your congregation to emulate. Each has its own particular strengths, gifts, and challenges. I visited congregations, of pastors I knew and many I did not, that were on route as I traveled about the country during my sabbaticals, parts of summers, and some weekends. One congregation's ministry cannot be a role model for another. Each congregation is blessed and struggling, special and unique and complex.

Neither are these congregations statistically representative of the entire church body. But they are varied—large and small, well-established and just being planted. By God's grace, each in its particularity is the church in that location and also part of God's whole church, the body of Christ. These congregations are not the best or worst churches, whatever that might mean. In congregational life we are frequently surprised when what we think is going well turns sour, and when that in which we have seen no life, springs forth in fruitful mission. My purpose was to learn from the people of God I met, to appreciate them, give thanks to God for them, and share their joys as well as their fears. I visited over ninety congregations. Not all appear in this book. The story of any congregation could be written here, including your congregation. I hope the questions placed throughout the chapters will help you think about your own stories. As part of the Lutheran Voices series, this book of congregational voices may help you hear your own voice more clearly.

When our son Joel was about two years old, he learned to do the finger play, "Here's the church, here's the steeple, open the doors, and see all the people." (He added, "And look, here they come to our house" because we lived in the parsonage next door.) Those words came to me on one trip while I was driving the many miles across Kansas. Whatever the location, each church is "here" to the people in that place. I discovered that people of all ages and backgrounds, and from all parts of the country, knew this children's finger play. So it became the framework for the four parts of the book.

Where is the church, and what is it really? What images and symbols describe it? How do the many word images for church that appear in the New Testament manifest themselves in congregations today? No matter if they are one block off Main Street or in the center of things, congregations need to know they are members together of the body of Christ. Communities change; mission remains.

What "steeples" and centers of meaning shape our society? Looking out the upstairs window from our grown-up son Joel's home today, I can see the steeple of Holy Family Church amid television towers and satellite dishes. Some church steeples no longer dominate the skyline; others are visible up the road from miles away. Where do people who live in a complex society with multiple pursuits of happiness look to find meaning and community?

How wide open are our church doors? Churches are challenged to find ways to open their doors wider for evangelical outreach. I visited congregations opening their doors to people who had not yet moved into their neighborhood. I also heard stories of congregations that were forced to close their doors or were afraid they might have to close them soon. The Reverend Linda Keeter Schultz, in her senior seminary approval interview, spoke about opening the doors of the church to let people in, but also to let them out, out into the world for ministry and mission.

How do we cherish the people? I saw so many examples of congregational members faithfully loving each other and reaching out in consistent care to the communities around. We need to really see one another, especially across racial and socioeconomic barriers. The Reverend Margaret Payne, bishop of the New England Synod of the Evangelical Lutheran Church in America, told me, "It's hard for us to understand that when we aren't deeply welcoming to people of other cultures—even if we are 'nice'—people will sense it and not tell us, but simply not come back."

Everywhere I went, in all kinds of churches, I met people who really wanted to share God's love in the world, some in ways that take risks, but often in familiar ways, such as quilting. I met quilters across the land and sometimes sewed with them—from Unitarian Universalist women in Burlington, Vermont, to Lutherans in Clarkstown, Pennsylvania; from the artistic quilt designers in Tipton, Iowa, to the Knotty (you have to say that aloud) Ladies in Albuquerque, New Mexico. Women make quilts for global relief work and for their local communities. Often quilts lead to mission. And when through their giving quilters hear of more needs, mission leads to more quilting.

Everywhere, of course, I also saw congregations facing money issues. But contrary to some church consultants who stratify "at risk" congregations by size of their annual budget, I resonate with the Reverend Kathryn Gerking, assistant to the bishop of the Southeastern Iowa Synod of the ELCA, who asks, "How does that phrase end?" We must ask, at a deep level, "at risk for what?" Synods

of the ELCA have heartily grasped the joy of having a global companion church. But how might we more fully develop the concept of
accompaniment with congregations in our own neighborhood?
How might we become companions who learn from one another,
realizing that each congregation is at risk in some way and that
empowered by the Spirit, each is called to take risks for the sake of
the gospel?

The Reverend Paul Stumme-Diers, bishop of the Greater
Milwaukee Synod of the ELCA, described how each congregation
in that synod is in an intentional partnership with another congregation in a setting strikingly different from its own. Whether
inner city, suburban, rural, large, or small, we will not make it
alone. We should not try to be self-sufficient; we are sustained in
ministry through interdependence. When "they had come
together" at the time of his ascension, Christ told his followers
that they would receive the power of the Holy Spirit to be wit-
nesses to the ends of the earth (Acts 1:6-8). When "they were all
together," the day of Pentecost came and a church of all nations
was born (Acts 2:1-21).

No matter how different church buildings look, inside people
gather around Word and Sacrament. I experienced this unifying
reality most profoundly during one spring sabbatical journey. I
attended a worship planning meeting at a congregation in
Lawrence, Kansas, where people were engaged in lively discussion
on the upcoming season's texts and hymns. A month and a half and
thousands of miles later at a church service in Baltimore, Maryland,
I heard the Sunday lessons read, but I heard them differently,
remembering those brothers and sisters in Christ studying the same
texts in Lawrence. Lutherans are linked through their liturgy.

By God's grace and design we belong to each other.
Congregations, while confessing they are part of the whole church,
often become so involved in dealing with their own issues that they
are tempted to forget the church down the road. This was true

across the country. Each congregation had its own problems, whether struggling to meet the budget with fewer members or growing so fast they were running out of space. All of us face a challenging question: How might congregations in ever-greater ways learn from, connect with, and strengthen one another?

Bishop Stumme-Diers frequently tells a story that he says he heard from someone else, who heard it from someone else. It's probably changed in the telling; that's how stories go. Maybe you have heard or told a version of it too: A pastor used the finger play "Here's the church, here's the steeple" in the children's time during a worship service. The children were asked to put their two hands together, entwining their fingers that could open up to show the people. Too late the pastor noticed a child, a recent immigrant from Cambodia, who had lost one hand through the devastation of the proliferation of land mines. Those watching from the pews realized the child would not be able to put her two hands together. In that instant: awkwardness, discomfort, and embarrassment. Of course it was too late to take back the request. (Is it too late to take back the land mines?) But spontaneously a little boy said, "That's okay. We'll make the church together." And they did.

You might try it. Put one of your hands together with the hand of another. It is not as easy as clasping your own hands. The hands may be different in size, in color, or in age. But with some practice to move beyond the awkwardness, we can be a church together.

In my visits I often greeted people with words from the biblical epistles, "Grace to you and peace from God through our Lord Jesus Christ. I bring you greetings from the churches at . . ." (where I had just been). Or, I wrote to them after my visit, "I thank my God every time I remember you, constantly praying with joy for your sharing in the gospel from the first day until now. I am confident of this, that the one who began a good work among you will bring it to completion" (Philippians 1:2-6, paraphrased). Congregations today are open, living letters to one another as God strengthens each one's sense of identity and vocation.

About the writing and use of the book

So many congregations. So many people. One of the hardest things about writing this book was letting go of some of the stories. It is a small book and not all of the stories would fit within these covers. More important is making room for the people in your congregation and neighborhood to become part of the book. The key to unlocking the book is to use the questions for reflection and discussion. By focusing on issues in other contexts, we are sometimes able to talk more easily about important questions we face in our own settings.

The book might be read for one's own personal reflection. It might be used with a church council or an outreach committee. The questions in this book might help congregations to develop their own evangelism strategy. The book could be used in adult forums, church staff meetings, seminary classrooms, or in a ministerial cluster of congregations. People could read the whole book and talk about the questions in a meeting, a series of meetings, or in a retreat setting. Or they could read it chapter by chapter and discuss it throughout the year. I hope such conversations will lead to mission and ministry in the public world beyond the doors of the church.

The stories are arranged in chapters according to topic. I gathered them on many different trips. I drove most of the time, and sometimes I flew and then rented a car. There is something about driving into a town and even more about walking the neighborhood that cannot be achieved by flying overhead. I had conversations with all kinds of people from a wide range of faith communities. All the stories in this book except two (one Lutheran Church—Missouri Synod and one United Church of Christ) are about congregations of the Evangelical Lutheran Church in America.

In order to bring the reader up to the present in my portrayal of a congregation, I blend information from different conversations. Usually I do not mention pastors or other rostered leaders by name;

this book is about congregations. Sometimes I do refer to people in the congregation by name, changing them or not as appropriate. The privileged nature of some conversations needed to be honored by not publishing them in this book. All was not prettied up for this visitor. Pain and conflict are realities everywhere.

My role was not judge (as in restaurant testing), or judicatory leader, or even teacher (seminary professor)—but visitor. Guest. When I called to ask if I could stop by, absolutely no one said, "Don't come." I received such a warm welcome in each place that I found leaving difficult. I wanted to stay and find out how things turned out, but that was not my role. As I reconnected, often by phone, in the process of writing this book, I received an equally gracious response, often from a new pastor whom I had not even met. Conversations became ministry as they told me their stories. I give thanks for these amazing blessings.

I thank the congregations and their pastors and leaders for their time and gracious hospitality. I thank Daniel Gerrietts, student assistant, for his partnership in conversations and editorial assistance. He has now graduated and is serving as pastor in his first call. I appreciate Kathryn Gerking for reading the manuscript and offering wise insight, Mary McDermott, faculty secretary, and Mark Kvale and Martha Butzier for assistance. I thank Thrivent Financial for Lutherans for providing seminary professor sabbatical grants and the Lilly Foundation for financial assistance for some of my travels.

As always, I am grateful to Wartburg Seminary, where I have been privileged to teach for over twenty-five years, for their ongoing commitment to academic excellence and to partnership with the church, both local and global. I give thanks for congregations that have nurtured me through the years. Yes, there is pain and conflict as well as growth and challenge, but God's faithfulness remains. I am thankful for family, particularly my husband, Burton, our sons and their families, and for friendships that have sustained me through the years.

Completing this book was difficult, but not for the usual reasons. I didn't want to stop writing because I was enjoying the conversations. The stories were continuing. So it is with the church. By God's grace, the story of God's reconciling love and forgiveness continues. Thanks be to God.

1

Where Is the Church?

"Turn off the interstate ramp and go left onto 29th Street. Go east two miles. You'll drive by the church, so turn around and come back." As I wondered aloud about directions that assumed I would miss my destination, the pastor added, "We sit back a little."

Ascension on 29th Street

He was right! Ascension, Del City, Oklahoma, sits back beside an automotive repair shop, across from a cemetery, and two blocks past the Midwest Trophy Company. The church is accessible on the main road of a strip city of small businesses, gun shops and pawnshops, storage facilities, and used car lots, one after another. The church name *Ascension* is a reminder of Christ's words when he left the disciples: "Why do you stand looking up toward heaven?" (Acts 1:11). Those words help us carefully look at a particular place that issues a call to discipleship: "Look around and see. Here is the church!"

Where is the church? The church is both local and universal. Where two or three are gathered in the name of Christ, Christ is present. Because the church is the body of Christ, as we gather in a local congregation, we need to imagine that also present with us are all other members of the body of Christ who have lived throughout history and who now gather in local congregations around the world. The local church is never alone, isolated, or self-sufficient because it is always connected to the universal church. But the universal also implies the local. Without becoming localized and specific, the church does not exist.[1] The church is always on some "29th Street," and no matter how out-of-the-way or hard to find, it is the church. Jesus became incarnate in an out-of-the-way place, a manger in Bethlehem. "Where is the church?" is a commission from the ascended, yet ever present, Christ to look around and be disciples in this place.

Oklahoma City was the second largest city in the world geographically until some of the annexed land was released for incorporation into little cities like Del City (named after town site owner's daughter, Delphine). "Even if people could find the church easily," the pastor said after I had safely arrived, "I'm not sure we would be a neighborhood church anyway. After all, where is the neighborhood? Winding streets discourage thoroughfare. You have to study a map even to drive through the area. Fences seemingly protect property, but they keep people apart. You can't really 'walk the neighborhood.'"

As life today becomes increasingly stressful and complex, diverse possibilities for interaction are multiplied; alienation and isolation are intensified. Expressways promise quick transit to the public world, but often dissect neighborhoods. The secondary arteries, such as 29th Street, are not so much centers of community as they are linear commercial pathways isolating people in their vehicles. People find where they need to go, but rarely find one another for a communal life together.

"We don't get a whole lot of visitors to this congregation," the pastor said. But some people do seek out Ascension. Some members drive ten miles to the church because of its proclamation and teaching of God's grace and its way of worship.

People seeking help find Ascension. "With an A, we're first in the phone book," the pastor said. There are many homeless, hungry people. The bottom is still dropping out for the lowest, and some of the formerly middle class, unaccustomed to poverty, don't know where to find help. While we talked in the church office, a woman telephoned to say "thank you" for the help the church had given her the day before, as though on cue to illustrate the biblical account of the one among ten who was healed by Christ and returned to give thanks (Luke 17:11-19).

Del City's self-identity does not include people needing low-income housing, so none is built. More and more of the property becomes rental property. The crime rate is not as high as it used to be, but guns are still the way to settle things. Tinker Air Force Base is nearby, and a significant number of Ascension's members are connected to the base. There is a Memorial Day parade down 20th Street, and Ascension takes part.

Ascension struggles with numbers growing smaller and members growing older. "A few years ago we seriously considered relocating further south or east where there is new growth, but financially we couldn't do it," said the pastor. "But God has put us here on 29th Street for a reason. Our mission challenge is to discover or rediscover that reason."

Questions for reflection and discussion

1. Where is your congregation?

2. How is it viewed by those who pass by?

3. How does your congregation feel about where it is located?

4. How do you picture the global and historic church present with you where you are?

St. Paul by the bridge

Where is the church? "The ministry of Word and Sacrament leads us to service in the world," summarized the pastor. "St. Paul congregation is called to be involved with the lives of people, proclaiming the gospel in whatever direction that may take us."

St. Paul's church building is at the very entrance of, almost under, the bridge over the Mississippi River in Clinton, Iowa, the most eastern point of the state. As I walked into the sanctuary I noticed it was pleasant, open, tall, and a bit formal. It felt established. A quick observation raised two possibilities: Either this was a church with bridges to the world or a relic of past significance with new societal bridges overarching the church, leaving it out of touch.

I had arrived at St. Paul about noon on a hot, Iowa July day, just in time for the pastor and associate in ministry to ask where I wanted to go for lunch. "Somewhere Clinton," I responded, which ruled out the Burger Kings and McDonalds whose ubiquitous presence signifies similarity rather than particularity among communities. We chose a downtown restaurant not far from the church. They told me the history of the congregation: The church has had three different names. In the beginning it was First English in an outreach effort to serve more than its predominant ethnic language group. It grew by leaps and bounds, becoming the largest church of its denomination in the city. Later it would become St. Paul's and finally just St. Paul.

Its vocation had been to be a church of the city, and the congregation stayed in its significant location. The area had been both downtown and neighborhood. But without changing its "where" the church was now in a different place. As the neighborhood changed, so did the church's well-established role. Lower economic residents live here now. Reaching out to them is a challenge from what looks like a formidable building. I could see the congregation takes the challenge seriously and does not want to merely patronize its downtown neighbors.

For years St. Paul has housed the local L'Arch group, an organization that provides adult living opportunities for people with developmental disabilities. Some of these individuals worship at St. Paul. One Sunday evening a month the congregation provides a community meal. Many homeless people and those with special needs look forward to this and have said, "It's like coming home."

Recently a man who is homeless and has a terminal illness had walked into the church during the week and said, "I don't know if I was ever baptized, and I want to be." Besides the church name, church buildings have invisible signs in front that may say things like, "You won't be able to find the door" or "We want you" or "We don't want you here." This man had "read" that the congregation was saying to him, "It's okay to come in." The pastor added, "We did baptize him."

It takes time for a church to gain a reputation of trust in a community. At St. Paul there are just enough people with passion for social ministry that they draw other people in to participate. The congregation has strong liturgy, music, and the arts that say, "Something important is going on here."

The day would turn out to be very warm, not just because of the temperature but because of the exciting ministry I observed coming from this formal, even "cool" looking church. Vacation Bible school was in progress from 9:30 until 2:30. Experiential education included going out into the community to visit shut-ins. I sensed that outreach is not only a long-term commitment, but also an everyday, well-established practice of "going where the gospel takes us," as one member said. This congregation is also very accessible to Clinton community events, which allows people to come through the door and become acquainted with St. Paul and its people.

A pattern was emerging: becoming involved, listening, learning, helping through the strengths St. Paul already has, and reaching out in new ways with new partnerships. "What is an image of ministry here?" I inquired. "A multifaceted ministry like a kaleidoscope," was the quick response. I followed up, "Like the ones with colored glass inside or the kind you look through at the world?" "Some of both!" At the center is the traditional Word and Sacrament ministry, with the multicolored facets of Scripture, music, and the arts. Looking out and being involved with the everchanging facets of the world is important, too. The congregation has had its struggles and will in the future; however, they are very much a part of the city. St. Paul's location is not changing, but their call to mission is. St. Paul continues to discern who they are, where they are, and the facets of their vocation.

New birth at Nativity

"Brandon, Georgie, Rachel, do you desire to be baptized?" The three children each said, "I do." "George, do you desire to be baptized?" "I do," the father answered. Tears came down the wife's face. Only the grandmother and the pastor knew that the father would request baptism along with his children this Sunday morning.

Nativity congregation is experiencing new birth through baptisms of new members. The older, aging congregation, which had been in the center of Commerce City, Colorado, in many ways had been unhealthy. They would either move and be reborn, or they would die. Now, with a move to what seems like "country" (although it is within the Denver metropolitan area), they are experiencing new health and are prepared to grow again. Substantial growth may take a while because they are seemingly way out in the country at 12500 East 104th Avenue. I could see nothing around but empty plots of ground. The texts for this Lenten Sunday focused on grains of wheat falling into the ground and dying. Still technically in Commerce City, the church will already be rooted when five thousand new houses are built all around. The new location is on the main thoroughfare to the new Denver international airport and right between the old part of Commerce City and Brighton, which does not have an ELCA congregation. Nativity is newly planted in the center of what is going to be. It has opened its doors and put flyers on distant houses four times already. Families are coming.

I experienced rich worship, good music, and solid biblical preaching the Sunday I visited. The cross outside stands tall, brought from the old building. Nativity deliberated for five years about where they should be. The pastor said, "The old building was dark—in some ways like a dungeon. So we intentionally built with all kinds of windows and natural light. That has made a huge difference in atmosphere and attitude." The congregation talked about changing their name with the new location. After prayer and much deliberation they decided: "Nativity is part of our history and of who we are now."

Four years later: The pastor, who has been on the journey with the congregation for twelve years said, "People are now living in houses a quarter mile away from the church, and construction of new homes has begun right across the highway. We've begun to experience growth. We continue mass mailings and door-to-door calling, as well as word-of-mouth messages that Nativity is here. Some simply see the church as they drive by. We went Christmas caroling in a new neighborhood. Evangelism is a lot of work, but also a lot of fun. And the Spirit is at work in the people. They are excited about inviting others."

New members are not simply transfers from other Lutheran congregations. The majority of people out here either grew up in the church and for some reason quit going or are entirely new to church. The pastor said, "We frequently hold new member classes, but I also ask people if they want to meet with me personally over lunch or dinner. I listen to questions they have that they are not comfortable asking in a group. Some say they wish they had heard about Christ when they were children. Many have not learned the basics of the Bible. I assure them that even folks who have been Lutheran from birth have much to learn about the Bible. We are all in the church together, learning from one another."

I asked, "And what about the neighborhood you left?" It would be easy to forget the old in excitement over the new. But she emphatically responded, "We did not do that! We were very intentional not to leave behind that part of Commerce City, a place of high industry and high crime. We are still very much a part of things. With a Roman Catholic parish, each Good Friday we walk the way of the cross through the old part of Commerce City. We invite the entire community and about two hundred people walk together. We continue to be part of Memorial Day commemorations, and I attend business and professional groups. We are involved with the school district. Some of our benevolence money goes to the Community Health Services. Our Sunday school makes and delivers a wholesome meal for the battered women and children's shelter each month."

Nativity is responding to Christ's mandate to go out into all the world and make disciples, "baptizing them in the name of the Father and of the Son and of the Holy Spirit" and teaching them (Matthew 28:19-20). In remembering that Christ is with them "to the end of the age," they care about the people where they have been, those where they are now, and those who are yet to come.

Questions for reflection and discussion

1. How has the area around your church building changed over the years?

2. Imagine looking out your church windows through a kaleidoscope into the world? What do you see?

3. What are the needs of the neighbors? How do you follow the gospel mandate to "go into the all the world" from where you are?

4. How do you discern your congregation's vocation?

Grace in Concord

In Concord, North Carolina, a city of fifty-eight thousand, African Americans make up over 15 percent of the population. Virtually all of them live in the southwest quadrant of the city. Grace Church, in that quadrant, is now 120 years old. I arrived early Saturday evening, and I could hear the music! My hosts and I went to the church, where the choir was practicing. Here I found an intense loyalty to the congregation. Every fall there is a Harvest Home, a huge festival, "bigger than Christmas," during which members come home to the parish to celebrate the anniversary. We walked through the Holtsen Education Center, fondly named after a pastor who served Grace for thirty-five years. Education has always been an important ministry of this congregation because public school integration came to Concord as late as 1964.

Historically, the segregated schools for black children were grossly underfunded. German Lutherans saw that their mission included providing quality education for African Americans. Grace congregation members started schools in its early years. (Sunday school children in the North sent their donations to help.) On the lower floor was a grade school and on the upper level was a college. Concerned about education, African Americans brought their children to these schools; many became Lutheran Christians. Later the college was moved to Greensboro to become the denomination's first African American seminary.[2]

That warm, spring evening we walked and then drove slowly around the community, stopping often to visit. Among the many small homes where people live close together in the southwest quadrant, some black professional people have built larger homes, choosing to stay in this largest and oldest African American community in Cabarrus County.

We went by the Logan Center. That's where the black public school had been, closed by the city fathers when integration occurred. The congregation's leadership had fought to keep a couple of buildings there, one of which is now a daycare center and the other a community center. For years Grace's pastor held Bible classes there: Thursday morning, Thursday evening, and Friday afternoon—one for each shift from the mill.

This town still ran on mill time: 7:00 A.M. to 3:00 P.M., 3:00 P.M. to 11:00 P.M., and 11:00 P.M. to 7:00 A.M. It made sense to run on mill time because everything that could not be nailed down had been owned by the textile mill owners. The large mansions in Concord had been for the mill owners; the middle managers had owned homes on streets to each side. The vast majority of people lived in small mill houses. The mill had owned the library, city hall, all the utilities, and 70 percent of the houses.

But things have changed. Concord is becoming a bedroom community for Charlotte. Textile mills have steadily closed over the years with jobs going overseas. Recently the largest mill in nearby Kannapolis closed. Other companies that came to the area have since closed, too, leaving forty-five hundred people in the county without jobs. Many people with financial burdens call on the social ministry of the churches.

In Concord there are other churches of the Lutheran tradition, though a different denomination. In the past fifteen years, probably two hundred Anglo Americans moving to Concord called to inquire about church services at Grace. But when they discovered the church was African American, they "found they could go to the other denomination after all." The pastor tried for a while to reach out to the Anglo Americans, but found his outreach not welcome. "Whites would be welcome here," he said, but the new white arrivals were professional and middle management people, and the boundaries that kept the races and classes apart for over a century keep the churches separate and segregated to this day.

Whereas Anglo American Christians in the United States often separated—and perhaps still separate—their private faith from their public daily life, African American Christians—denied "public" access—used biblical narrative to create a communal public life for themselves. This faith life gave them strength for daily existence. African American churches provided acceptance and opportunities for skill and leadership growth. People took responsibility for meeting their needs for education, recreation, and association in civic clubs within the boundaries of their life together. The question, "Where is the church?" coincided with "Where is daily life?"

Integration provided access to public education and services for African Americans, but ironically also meant loss of their power base and centers of community. We drove past the black cemetery, the black funeral home, a black American Legion Hall. (There are no bars here; this is a dry county.) But there is no public school here now, no swimming pool, and no library.

Where is the church? In Concord, North Carolina, Grace church is where it has been for 120 years: in the center of its black community—gathering, educating, leading, caring—poised at the fringe of the broader community of Concord. There is sadness, tragedy, and scandal in this; paradoxically there is life and growth and joy as well. That's Grace. Later Sunday afternoon we walked through the invisible barriers, along a street into the rest of the town.

Questions for reflection and discussion

1. What are the visible or invisible lines of separation between races, classes, and ethnic or religious groups in your community? Where is your congregation?

2. Is your congregation a place of communal life? What sounds of celebration can be heard from your church?

3. To what particular needs has your congregation responded historically? What needs are emerging today?

4. Here's the church! Where in the world is your church?

2

What Is the Church?

A quiet town by anyone's standards, Daykin, Nebraska, offered shelter from the January cold. I arrived after dark. The long winter night might have hidden the town, but it didn't. The church is here and has been for a long time. Church and town simply are! An hour southwest of Lincoln, this might be a place where people would want to escape to the country. "Most of those people have not discovered Daykin yet," the pastor said with a twinkle in her eye.

Hidden away? Not yet discovered? No matter! Looking through the eyes of the people, one sees a steady, stable identity to sustain them through the dry seasons and winds of change.

Disciples in Daykin

Daykin, Nebraska, is known as "the windmill capital," an identity that conveys grain and wind, energy and transition. Daykin struggles with grain prices and changing times. Among the windmills—most are actually gone—is the church steeple. St. John's Lutheran struggles along with the people; however, its symbol of identity remains strong.

The people of St. John's Lutheran Church are dependable, much like the biblical image of "salt of the earth." There are more than eighty images of the church in the New Testament, some more prominent than others, but none paramount. The church is "sign," "fish," "boat," "vineyard," God's planting," and much more. The four major images are "people of God," "the new creation," "the fellowship of faith," and "the body of Christ."[1]

The church steeple among the windmills of Daykin is like a "fellowship of faith" where the saints walk daily with the Spirit for witness and ministry. Believers are bound together, independent yet interdependent. The mutuality in joy and in suffering intersects all human relationships. They have always watched out for each other. They handle conflict carefully because they know they will have to live with these people all of their lives.

Even in the January cold, I could feel the warmth of this place. After giving me time to relax from the strenuous drive over icy roads, the pastor fed me a hearty soup and wholesome muffins. You don't need much of that kind of food to feel you are well fed.

We talked for a while after supper and then went to visit the neighbors Erwin and Gladys. At hearing the sounds of those names, the pastor's dog was ready to go. Evidently both pastor and her dog often had been to the home of Erwin and Gladys for Sunday dinner. In fact, the dog knows everyone in town.

"The congregation is smaller than it used to be," Erwin measured.

"As farms get larger, farmers get fewer." With those words, Gladys had somehow said it all.

"We lost our farm." The words came simply, as though they might as well say what was so central to their lives. We talked about the weather for a while, not as a diversion; weather and farming go together. Erwin went on, "The snow is good this year but we're still very low on moisture. We're 70 to 75 percent irrigated, but irrigation pays off most when you don't need it." Each year farming is a risk.

How did this fellowship of faith react? "At first we felt isolated. Some people simply didn't know what to say so they didn't say anything. But they cared."

Christians confess belief in Jesus Christ, who was isolated and abandoned on the cross, who rose from the dead to new life, and sought the company of his disciples.[2] Christians believe in the Holy Spirit, who created and is sustaining the church. The Pentecost account concludes with a picture of the new church: "They devoted themselves to the apostles' teaching and fellowship, to the breaking of bread and the prayers. . . . All who believed were together and had all things in common; they would sell their possessions and goods and distribute the proceeds to all, as any had need" (Acts 2:42, 44-45). Our task as disciples is not primarily to admire or critique the church, or to believe in it, but rather to believe the church is God's gathering, here, in this place.[3]

The consolidated school is not in Daykin, but nearby. People wonder how long the school will stay open because there are fewer and fewer children. Children are more precious than gold here. There is a nice, new bank in town, the "People's Bank." The lumberyard and hardware store are flourishing. Across from St. John's is a grain elevator. It's a co-op branch, no longer home owned. One looks around in the daylight and sees prosperity, but it's an illusion because banks own most everything.

St. John's in Daykin is family oriented. Christmas celebrations begin three weeks early because of trying to arrange all the various extended family gatherings. There is a surplus of family—an assumption of family. A new single person in town—a teacher, a pastor—is not unwelcome. It's just hard to know how to welcome a stranger when people have never been one.

The boundary of the church is not the edge of town or the school district, but the intricate interrelatedness of extended families. But to say the image of the church is a "family" is to convey only the romanticized view of family; while comforting to some it can also exclude.

Having seen the church through the eyes of its members, I was eager to go inside the building. It was ornate, yet simple and sturdy like the people. The congregation is a visible sign of invisible grace. The congregation does not live beyond its means. They know who they are in this place and that there may not be growth in numbers or wealth. They care for each other and give generously to the needs of the church beyond their community. Even when they were without a pastor for three years, benevolences did not drop.

From time to time the steeple bell tolls, as it has for years, becoming a herald to the town at the time of someone's death—one stroke for each year of life. When it tolls a long time, people understand, but there is a pervasive sadness when it tolls only a few times. The church steeple symbolizes both a profound understanding of death and a sturdy desire to live. I could clearly see that.

Questions for reflection and discussion

1. What are the sights and sounds of the church (or churches) where you live?

2. What biblical image of the church, for example, "vine and branches," "rock," "one loaf," "salt of the earth" describes your congregation?

3. How do people where you live connect with one another? When do they feel isolated or abandoned?

4. How does the image your church has of itself shape the way they care for one another? For those beyond their church?

Peace in Peoria

I drove west on Thunderbird Road, out further and further into the desert, past affluent signs of new, large car dealerships in this third-ring suburb of Phoenix. Peace Lutheran in Peoria, Arizona, has a lovely, desert-colored edifice built in the late 1990s. Now with over eleven hundred baptized members, seven hundred gather for worship on Sunday. The sanctuary felt like the biblical image of the church as "new creation." In fact, there is a creation window in the front through which one can see out to the world. On the outside wall is a simple, large cross. Although many new churches in their name, symbols, and worship life omit or downplay the "gloomy part" of a suffering God who suffers with us, Christ's cross is central to Peace.

Peace and Peoria are still growing. I saw tracks of desert, checker-boarded with new condominiums and single-family homes, all seemingly the same desert color. The desert seems to sense people have arrived; the stress on water is great.

The pastor has been here for thirteen years, and his leadership has certainly helped this congregation grow. But the identity of this congregation is not all about the pastor, and his picture isn't the first thing one sees on the Web site. It is all about shared ministry—solid, energetic, vibrant, holistic ministry. The church image here is not one of focusing primarily on being large for the sake of being large. Nor is the image full-service church, which in this consumer-oriented culture tends to focus primarily on having personal needs of the members met. I saw an integrated ministry of administration, learning community, preaching, sacraments, and care.[4]

The worship life is "informal traditional," clearly bearing the marks of the historic liturgy. Holy Communion is celebrated at every service; fourteen musical groups incorporate the varied gifts of this large congregation. Small groups meet to pray for one another. Spirituality among these Christians is not individualistic, but personal, real, and corporate.

It was Friday morning, and the preschool children gathered in the sanctuary for worship. What a joy to hear them sing and see teachers and pastor tell the biblical story of the lost sheep. To help affirm the promises of baptism, the congregation provides educational opportunities from early childhood through high school graduation and beyond. Educational ministry is an intergenerational celebration of community. Institutional growth at Peace Lutheran is rooted in education. All new members, whether lifelong Lutherans or people totally new to the Christian faith, together attend "growing disciples" classes.

Lifelong learning needs to help people wrestle with difficult ethical questions. Currently about 150 people from five congregations in their Cactus Conference are using the ELCA study on human sexuality, recognizing the varieties of ways Christians interpret scripture in relation to ethical issues.

Congregational growth is all about empowering people to share their gifts and setting them free to serve. "By the grace of God this congregation has become generous with time, money, and our facilities," said the pastor. In this affluent area the church budget is large: $900,000. They give $200,000 away. "Here's the church" is not limited to the person next to them in the pew. The pastor said, "It means being connected with congregations in their neighborhood, their synod, across the country, and around the world." That means co-sponsoring a Lutheran thrift store devoted to mission outreach, helping feed hungry people each Sunday in central Phoenix, and purchasing Fair Exchange coffee, which helps transform the lives of coffee farmers in Tanzania. All of this is countercultural in a time and place where people are urged to secure their own retirement in the sun and to live and consume in isolated comfort, viewing the world beyond as a threat to be avoided or invaded.

People need hands-on experiences to learn a discipleship of care: Stephen Ministries training, monthly youth service projects, the Thursday morning mens Bible study group's recent trip to build houses in Mexico. Many others in the congregation prayed for their journey and now know they need to go next time. I was told, "Here, in this cultural context, we need to teach compassion."

I heard the people of Peace talk comfortably, naturally, about their faith. Church council members tell their faith stories at council meetings. This area of fast, new growth presents different ministry challenges than areas of the country from which many of these people came. For some, their lives have been totally reoriented, not just because of moving here, but because of their new or renewed relationship to Christ. "It is sometimes painful growth," one said, "but we see the Spirit at work."

We ate lunch at a nearby golf course. Where else? In Phoenix you are always near a golf course. With reasonable prices and a beautiful view, the restaurant is a place to meet people. Tumbleweed blew across the road as we returned from lunch. The desert is still here.

Questions for reflection and discussion

1. How are the challenges of faithful discipleship different in areas of growth or loss in population? How are they the same?

2. What strikingly different images of the church have you seen in your life? How can we move beyond mere admiration, envy, critique, or complaint, to see the church in all its different forms and varying calls to vocation in the world?

3. How does seeing the church "beyond the person sitting beside you in the pew" change not only the scope of mission but one's very concept of what is the church?

Where in Worcester?

Another significant image of the church in the New Testament is "body of Christ." I encountered that image of body when I searched for a missing limb, Iglesia Luterana San Juan congregation. Where in Worcester, Massachusetts, was it anyway?

I had been there. I had seen the funeral home that was now a church, on a high hill in the center of town. I had seen the worship space filled with cribs for the daycare of infants during the week. How fitting, all these newly born babies in a former parlor for the dead.

Three women—a teacher/administrator, a social worker, and a pastor—had welcomed me during my visit: Miriam, Luz, and Rafaela. Such strong, caring Hispanic women. They talked in the different voices of their various areas of expertise, yet they talked as one. This partnership was their leadership. Body of Christ!

The building was filled with life all day, every day: teenage mothers, people learning English as a second language, people studying for their GED certificate. The church served the neighborhood, including Vietnamese, African Americans, and more. When people needed social services they looked to San Juan to help them find it.

San Juan, a bilingual, multicultural mission, was begun in 1980 and organized as a congregation in 1986. After an eleven-month vacancy early on, "God sends us this woman," said Miriam. "We feel support from the church, especially from our partner congregations." Body of Christ!

A fourth woman, Ruth, was part of this story, too. An associate in ministry, Ruth had hosted me the day before at Immanuel Lutheran Church in Holden, Massachusetts, right outside of Worcester. Immanuel was vitally connected with San Juan. What had begun as a financial partnership became much more. Some Holden members began taking the check to San Juan rather than merely sending it. One noted, "Our church is formal; here you seem so friendly." Ruth, a strong leader at Immanuel, linked people together in the body of Christ.

A church that was friendly—and vivacious and tenacious. A church's identity fuels its mission and its mission shapes its identity. San Juan fought for good housing for poor people and provided legal and social services and education. Gospel action and gospel proclamation were vitally intertwined. "This is what the church can be," I thought. San Juan had eighty-one baptized members and more who, though not members, participated. I discovered outreach to be contagious. San Juan served Latino people from all over Worcester.

One member said, "I was lacking something in my life. Then I met Pastor at a community meeting and I thought, 'One of these days I will go there.' Miriam, who was my neighbor, pestered me until I went and, when I did, I said, 'My God, this is my church!' I had been missing my culture and language. When I was ill, I didn't know to express my pain in English. It's not the same feeling."

Another told me, "I was born in New York City; my mother is from Puerto Rico. At school everything was in English; at home everything in Spanish. As an adult, my personhood was in the middle: feeling in Spanish and thinking in English. Then I was invited to an anti-racism workshop held at Immanuel Lutheran in Holden. I thought, 'The Lutheran Church must be a church that cares about such things.' I began to visit San Juan in my neighborhood and now I am a member. The church needs to be a safe place, physically and emotionally, to truly be ourselves."

A church may have an inclusive stance, but not an inclusive reality. "I kept looking for a place that didn't have a double standard. Either we are all equal and try to live God's word or we shouldn't open the doors. When we present ourselves as an inclusive church, that must mean an ever widening circle," said Miriam.

But where was that ever-widening circle now, a few years later? Why couldn't I find San Juan in Worcester today?

I made some phone calls, which led me to a fifth woman, Ann, present pastor at Concordia Lutheran, just a few blocks from where I had visited the church-in-a-funeral-home. Ann told me San Juan no longer existed as a separate congregation. She told me Rafaela was now serving a congregation in Connecticut. A few more phone calls. A few years ago the synod mission board at that time closed San Juan because it couldn't be totally self-sustaining. Percentage-wise these members of limited means had been giving more than many of their counterparts elsewhere, but the total had been still too little.

I was saddened to hear that.

With a "body of Christ" image of the church, however, the story of one congregation is always entwined with other stories. Concordia is a stalwart congregation—a stone building with a rich German heritage. Over twenty years ago, the pastor at that time invited one Puerto Rican man to Concordia. That man brought others. With that nucleus the synod mission board had decided to develop a separate Hispanic mission, and San Juan was born. But after considerable struggle and the closing of San Juan congregation, a remnant came to Concordia.

Ann said, "We see the importance of having a congregation that reaches across racial and economic class lines." Today members of Concordia come from all over the world: Puerto Rico, Liberia, Ghana. Lutheran Immigration is resettling new immigrants here. "We do not romanticize the poor; we truly enjoy being together," she said. Each Friday night fifty to sixty children from the neighborhood come for education and community. "Many receive the Sacrament of Holy Baptism—and quite of few of those want to be acolytes," the pastor said. "We have a core of twenty-two acolytes in this relatively small church. Come and visit us on Sunday sometime!"

Questions for reflection and discussion

1. How have you experienced the church as "body of Christ"? How can congregations be connected and supportive of one another?

2. Who should determine whether a congregation should close? How can we be the body of Christ even when some parts of the body cannot be self-sustaining?

3. How does our image of "what" the church is affect the way we look at one another historically and globally?

4. How can being multilingual and multicultural enrich a congregation and its mission?

A myriad of images

The church is not merely the carrier of the gospel, a place to hear the good news; the church is gospel action. "For Christ's sake, the church is the reality of the alienated reconciled, the rebellious returned, the lonely encompassed with love."[5]

In my travels visiting congregations across this country, I asked, "What image of the church do you have?" Although an abstract question, people were always quick to respond: "a mustard seed," "an anchor," "a refuge." The pastor in Maquoketa, Iowa, and a number of others across the country replied: "a sleeping giant." A lay person explained: "We have so many gifts in this congregation. If people began to use them in their ministry in daily life, and together in this community, I believe we could really make a difference for justice."

What biblical images help you imagine what the church has been, is, and might be? What other contemporary images from your context come to mind? The church, justified by grace through faith, is liberated for mission. It is not that the church has a mission of salvation. Rather the mission of God includes the church; God creates and recreates the church as it lives through history engaged in God's mission.[6] Truly the church has many images. By God's continuing grace, forgiveness, and liberating, spirit-filled new life, enormous tasks await the church in this changed and changing world.

Another glance

I like to check back on congregations I have visited, particularly if those visits were early in my travels. I did so not only with San Juan, but also with St. John's in Daykin, Nebraska. Not a lot has changed there. The farm economy is still a challenge. St. John's is now yoked with a congregation eighteen miles down the road, St. Paul's in Gilead. (Yes there's a sign at the edge of town that says, "Balm.") The only business still going in Gilead is Pioneer Inn. There is no "no smoking" section in that bar and grill because no one in town smokes anymore.

Back in Daykin, Erwin has died; the bells tolled his long life. But Gladys still plays the organ at St. John's every Sunday, and she has warmly welcomed the new pastor, who had previously lived in large cities. The pastor told the people of Daykin, "You live in a beautiful place. My eyes can't open wide enough to take in so much beauty. Corn is dancing in the wind. I don't see this as a 'first-call' parish. This is my call, and I fully expect to be here ten years from now."

Both congregations struggle, but they are learning how to care about and have fun with each other. Two days before I called, on New Year's Eve, whole families from St. Paul's and St. John's had a "lock-in" all-night party. No one slept much! At 11:30 they had a worship service to welcome in another new year, and everyone got a chance to ring the bells.

3

All Kinds of Steeples

"Here's the church, here's the steeple." Steeples of great cathedrals and of small country churches rise above their landscape, signaling praise of God. Many other God-created and human-constructed statues, monuments, and spires press skyward as well, symbolically saying, "Here's the steeple on which to focus your attention." Throughout my travels I looked for and took pictures of all kinds of steeples rising to the sky.

The cherry blossoms in Washington, D.C., arrived early the March I followed the spring north from Alabama to New England. I viewed the Washington Monument and Lincoln Memorial, so laden with meaning, through the soft beauty of flowering trees given to the United States by Japan decades ago. Across the fertile farms of Indiana, Illinois, Iowa, and into the plains states of Kansas, Nebraska, and the Dakotas, grain elevators symbolize food for the world and a way of life. I can still see the elevator looming into the sky, dwarfing the town of Rudd, Iowa, and the wheat elegantly painted on the side of an elevator along with the words: Hereford, Texas.

So many steeples. So much to ponder about the sources and expressions of identity, worth, and meaning: the Saturn V launch vehicle at the United States Space and Rocket Center in Huntsville, Alabama; the Golden Gate Bridge (I walked partway across, noting the telephone help lines for people who are tempted to jump from that great height); Mt. Rushmore—more "patriotically" embellished with sound and light then ever; and the nearby monument to the Native American leader, Crazy Horse, yet incomplete.

Great towers carry electricity from Hoover Dam, especially westward. Utility lines for a power-hungry society were everywhere; this is an environmentally unaware culture. I climbed the steps to state capitol buildings—Concord, New Hampshire; Montpelier, Vermont; Madison, Wisconsin; Des Moines, Iowa—working monuments, accessible to the people they represent.

Some towers are powerful; others whimsical, such as the tall sign outside of Dickinson, Texas, for an establishment known far and wide: "Heartbreakers." This gentleman's club, on the road between Houston and Galveston, had been the focus of local news—so, yes, I did have to look inside. And right next to it on property owned by a local church the sign: "Jesus mends broken hearts."

There are steeples with crosses and those with a stake—the grand Mormon cathedrals of Salt Lake, San Diego, and St. George, Utah. More magnificent than any human edifice were the red rocks of the high desert and, of course, those highest of steeples across this land, the Rocky Mountains themselves.

You can't miss those hamburger golden arches not only across America but spread throughout the world. You can spot them anywhere and know precisely what they promise. But they take second place to the St. Louis Arch itself, gateway to westward expansion. Going to the top is impressive; so is viewing the old courthouse that the arch frames. There the Dred Scot case was tried as this nation struggled with the legality of slavery.[1]

What do all of these "steeples" mean? And where is the church steeple in the midst? Some years ago St. John's Lutheran Church in the heart of Manhattan sold their valuable land for the sake of mission and ministry. A skyscraper rises above while their vibrant congregation worships below at ground level, reaching out to the jazz community and being advocates for social justice.

I climbed up and looked out from a church steeple in Cheshire, Connecticut, nostalgically seeing Sleeping Giant State Park, a great bluff—that looks like a giant asleep—that as a family we had climbed many times years ago when our children were young. What a view!

And so I ponder: What do they all mean? Commerce and community, power and opportunity, history and dreams for the future. People are drawn to them, miss them when they are gone—the site of the twin towers in lower Manhattan continues to be a place of mourning and memory for the lives lost there—and continue to erect them.

Questions for reflection and discussion

1. Look around. What are the significant "steeples" in your area? What are the focal points as you enter or leave your community or observe in the midst of daily life? How do they orient people's sense of place, meaning, and worth?

2. What is the place of the church steeple in your community? How is it viewed by people? Whether or not your church building has one, what might "here is the steeple" mean to you and to people in your congregation?

3. How is the view of or from these steeples in your community changing? What is your personal viewpoint?

Monument Avenue in Richmond

Monument Avenue in Richmond, Virginia, is the site of First English Lutheran Church, a "tall steeple" church.[2] I took a picture of its twin towers. I also took a picture looking out through the cut glass narthex window onto Monument Avenue and saw the back end of a statue of General J. E. B. Stuart on his horse. Stuart is significantly facing south, his horse rearing—some say to show he died in battle. Further up the avenue is General Robert E. Lee's monument. The horse has all feet on the ground; Lee died a natural death. (Some say whether the general faces north or south signifies if he lived or died in battle.) Up the avenue the monuments go, "steeples" all, memorials to a dream that never quite came to be.

First English is a metropolitan congregation, not a downtown or inner city church. It was founded in 1869, first as St. Mark's, but soon renamed First English to let people know they were not worshiping in a foreign language: "If you are Lutheran and you are here in Richmond, we want to reach out to you." Richmond is Baptist country. The pastor from 1906 to 1956 thought it was important to build a Lutheran church of public prominence in this proud, historic city, and so they did at Stuart Circle on Monument Avenue.

Heavy granite, Gothic outside, the sanctuary feels Victorian. For many years First English was the only church of its denomination in Richmond. Membership was about twelve hundred until the post-World War II move to the suburbs. Today First English is going though revitalization, saying once again, "We are here, and we want to reach out to you." They daringly yet willingly took out pews in the middle of their beautiful sanctuary to accommodate wheelchairs. (They didn't think people with disabilities should be in the back of the church.) And much more is going on inside.

But first we needed to go outside and walk the area. There are five churches near Stuart Circle: United Church of Christ, Lutheran, Presbyterian, Episcopalian, and Roman Catholic. Refusing to compete to see "which steeple is taller," since the 1970s they have served together in an ecumenical alliance that they refer to as "Stuart Circle Parish." They share social ministry outreach. Each Palm Sunday, I was told, together they parade down Monument Avenue amidst steeples of war, defeat, regional identity, and pride, carrying the church's center—the cross.

We walked among stately homes on broad, tree-lined streets. Although the area has struggled, it is definitely on the rise economically. We talked with people. "I'm the pastor of First English," said my companion to a middle-aged couple we met. "Yes, we've heard," the woman responded. She went on, "We live in this neighborhood on purpose, because we want to live near the people we serve." She is with social services of the Commonwealth of Virginia; he is a teacher.

Others came by, walking their dogs, stopping to chat. It seemed the streets were filled with newcomers in this heart of the old confederacy. Most could obviously live in the suburbs if they chose. That was not true for other residents. I saw some adult homes in the old mansions, such as "Mrs. Buchanan's," places where elderly people live together, which provide financial and social support as they shape their life in community. In other homes a supervisor lives with those who are mentally ill or who otherwise might be homeless.

First English is committed to a ministry of inclusivity beyond Monument Avenue. This is the "fan" area of Richmond, so named because streets fan out from the center of the city. I pictured the many ministries of First English fanning out as well. First English opens its doors for the parish Sunday afternoon meal ministry sponsored by Stuart Circle Parish. They provide space and support for the Read Center, an adult literacy program known all over Richmond. They started an adult day care center that soon outgrew its space. During the cold season, January to March, people from First English volunteer at the United Church of Christ across Stuart Circle that serves as an intake center for homeless people who stay on the fringes of downtown. Those who are homeless can walk to Stuart Circle and then are transported to suburban churches that have space for this "cot ministry."

First English welcomes students from Virginia Commonwealth University, which is within walking distance. Members work closely with the Inner Faith Campus Ministry. Many young people are looking for churches with historical integrity and traditional worship and music. People come to First English because of the rich worship combined with vital social ministry, social ministry sponsored by the congregation as well as through the involvement of its members in their ministries in daily life. The congregation uses words used by many urban congregations of the ELCA around the country: "In the City for Good" and adds—"Making a Difference."

The pastor said, "We have to continually rethink our mission as we live into God's promised future."

The identity of First English members is not in its towers. They do not simply think, "I'm a member of a big church in an important place." But the church is special to them, as they appreciate its traditions and reach out from their towers to people among the monuments.

The monument in Grand Junction

"Grand Junction is not Denver," I was told up front. "We do things our way, not Denver's way." In no way had I assumed this was Denver. In fact, my journey across the mountains had been the most difficult driving of the past six weeks, not because of the mountains themselves—we do live in an age of interstate highways. But I had left the spring blossoms of the eastern slopes and run headlong into a late winter (well, spring) blizzard at the pass. I stopped to wait out the storm in Dillon by sitting for awhile in a local ski/snowboard shop (and bookstore), then in a laundromat, and finally in a restaurant. When I heard the storm might not let up for two more days, I figured I could either wait it out or see it through. I decided to take my chances with the truckers. I didn't just see the Rockies, I experienced them: fog, clouds, snow, ice. Through Vail Pass, I descended the western slopes to be embraced by a beautiful, warm March afternoon in Grand Junction.

It was Palm Sunday weekend. Early Saturday evening my host took me up on the Colorado National Monument, a steeple. It is a monolith, a rock form shaped through erosion all around. From there we could view the Grand Mesa and Book Cliffs that ring the northern end of the valley. I could see Mt. Garfield in the distance.

American Lutheran was started at the time of World War II. Like many churches of that era, it took its name from its denomination, but also with an overtone of the heightened patriotism of the day. Today people come here to bike, ski, hike, and fish. They take their leisure seriously. To minister here, one needs to be where the people are, out of doors. It's a pastor's struggle not to take their weekend absences personally.

I asked people about the significant steeples of meaning in their lives. Where does faith fit in their week? I was told they hunger for meaning and belonging, and for a God worthy of being the rock-solid foundation in their lives. The next morning I experienced them being a solid community of faith. People of all ages serve weekly Eucharist. I loved hearing a distinctly older woman's voice: "Body of Christ given for you." Serving beside her was a boy in red sneakers.

Between services, Tinker came up and greeted me like a long-lost sister. We had met a few years before outside of San Francisco at a Women of the ELCA theological retreat. Tinker introduced me to other women, including one who told me she is deliberately seeking to live a simpler lifestyle, one that is not so demanding on the ecology. People here appreciate the environment. The co-chair of the congregation's executive committee for their capital campaign is an engineer working on clean-up after years of uranium mining. There is a research center in the community studying the incidents of lung disease because of the mining.

I stayed overnight at the parsonage in this neighborhood with many children. Emily at eight years of age had recently cut her long hair. On television she had seen human hair being used to make wigs for people recovering from cancer. It was Emily's idea to cut her hair and give it to those in need whom she did not know.

In this congregation, children's gifts are used. On Palm Sunday morning I watched children of all ages line up to process with their palm branches. The younger ones were a bit timid and the older ones a bit gangly, but all joined the parade, including guests and visitors. The latter may not have quite known what it was all about. (Those who processed on the first Palm Sunday didn't either.)

I saw other gifted people like the quilters. I heard the musical gift of a man who offered a solo at the beginning of each service. He sang as though he had seen the events of that first Palm Sunday himself. The gifts of each generation are needed in this and in every congregation.

In our contemporary society the concept of family is often likened to a pillar providing the one solid foundation for life.[3] But missing from this cultural icon is the need each family has for a broader faith community. One hears in the media that pressures seem to be eroding away the American monument of family. American Lutheran Church is intent on engaging in a counter-American cultural mission of inter-generational ministry. How are newcomers, such as the Latinos who labor seasonally in the fruit orchards in this grand valley—people from "other families"—welcomed into a congregation? People at American Lutheran care not only about "my family," but also about all God's children who are in our hands.

"Our congregation is growing," said the pastor, "and we believe we can grow even more if we have the space to facilitate community across generations. We've evaluated our strengths of ministry among children, families, and seniors and have purchased seven-and-one-half acres of land to relocate and expand." They want to build a solid community where people can find "grandparents" and "uncles" and "aunts" through faith. This is particularly necessary in an area of the country where many people are no longer near their families of origin. He said, "This is our vision, our calling."

My visit had come to an end. I drove off toward Utah knowing I would soon experience the beauty of the high desert. But before I left town I just had to climb Dinosaur Hill. There is something about a peak that invites me to climb.

Questions for reflection and discussion

1. How are these two congregations (First English and American Lutheran) similar to and different from each other? From your own?

2. How does the context of the community shape their ministry? Your own?

3. Given the traditions, sources of meaning, and needs of the community, how might your congregation refocus its evangelical outreach?

Far away steeples: Colorado Springs

NORAD, Pikes Peak, and the Air Force Academy chapel. Formidable steeples all!

Inside Bethel Lutheran in Colorado Springs people were gathering for a Wednesday evening potluck supper, confirmation class, and education time before Lenten services. I was warmly included in all. Christian education, weekly Eucharist, and strong new member classes are important here in what, I was told, may not be the Bible belt, but is surely the Bible "pocket" of the United States.

Before supper I had looked around the large church. The congregation had recently completed an extensive expansion, including a new sanctuary. Bethel can be clearly seen from the street, but a woman with whom I ate the Lenten supper said of their expansion, "The cross now is very visible on the outside. It looks more like a church than just a building on a hill."

The steeples that surround this city were still on my mind: NORAD, Pikes Peak and, not far to the north, the Air Force Academy chapel with its seventeen steeples. (Folklore says they represent the twelve disciples and the five senators who made possible the construction of the chapel).

The mountain, of course, was here first; it stands in solitary grandeur. When you see Pikes Peak, you cannot forget it. Although people use it for reference—west—and don't like it when, because of the weather, it can't be seen; at the same time, they take it for granted. This steeple will surely always be there. It can be appreciated another day.

NORAD (North American Aerospace Defense Command, built inside Cheyenne Mountain) and the Air Force Academy symbolize quite different kinds of steeples—steeples erected to honor and to further a nation's military power on earth and supremacy in the skies. The military industrial complex is core to the Colorado Springs economy and ethos. Academy Boulevard is the main north-south artery through the city.

I went into Bethel's sanctuary for the service. As I sat in the pew, my eyes were on the cross in the chancel. As I glanced to the side through the clear glass sanctuary windows I could also see the red lights of the communication towers of NORAD on a hillside much higher than Bethel's.

People, with their businesses, houses, and condos, now almost connect Denver and "The Springs" on the front range of the Rockies along that horizontal steeple, Interstate 25. But before I traveled north, I had to return as I always do when I am in Colorado Springs, to the city park that is Garden of the Gods. The quiet, statuesque beauty of these red rock formations is like none other.

Nearby steeples: Always in change

I live in Dubuque, Iowa, where I have taught for over twenty-five years in the castle-like seminary named Wartburg. It was designed to resemble the Wartburg Castle in Eisenach, Germany, where Martin Luther took refuge and translated the New Testament into the language of the people. I can look out from the third floor library windows and see the beautiful Iowa landscape to the West. I can climb to the top of the tower and see the mighty Mississippi River to the

East. As I drive up Fremont Avenue each morning on the way to the seminary, I see the full view of this "castle," neither an ivory tower nor a fortress from the world, but a place of communal worship and learning to equip leaders to go out into the world to serve.

Not far west of Dubuque, the steeple of St. John's Lutheran Church, north of Dunkerton, Iowa, was torn off and left crumpled at the rear of the old, white-framed church, when a half-mile wide tornado cut through the area. The church had just recently been remodeled.

East of Dubuque in nearby Galena, Illinois, a congregation added a steeple to a church building, which before "didn't look like a church."

Little Grandview Heights Baptist Church in Dubuque, Iowa, had been hidden from the street, set on a long driveway back from the avenue. While expressways sometimes cut parish neighborhoods in two, in this case, the new highway south of the city cut through the trees and bluff in a way that happened to open up a grand view of Grandview, not only from the highway but from the downtown beyond.

I wonder what steeples, tall on a bluff or not, you see in the course of a week. Whether steeples are falling or being added, churches and their steeples are in flux in a world that is always changing. Church steeples focus our hearts and minds on praise of almighty God. They signal stability and challenge, hospitality and mission.

St. John's in downtown Des Moines, Iowa, is across from Veterans Memorial Convention Center. The church steeple remains a landmark through years of urban change. With its "In the City for Good" sign bold and clear on the side of the building, the church continues to be a Lutheran presence, a gathering place for city and synodical worship. St. John's congregation continues to serve the community with music, lecture series, and powerful social ministry in the nearby inner city neighborhoods.

Not far south of Dubuque, Zion Lutheran (a steeple-like name) is in the center of things, too: Elvira, Iowa, an unincorporated town.

Its steeple signals strength and tradition. "The intersection of F12 and Z36 roads is the second busiest in the county," I was told. "People look up to the church" and see it as "a beacon of hope in a world of pain." Over the years, the members have put four additions on the building, to the "north, south, east, and west," for education, handicap accessibility, and social outreach, doing most of the work themselves. When a woman from a store in Davenport called to say UPS wouldn't deliver to that rural address, the pastor said it was at a main intersection. "Oh, that's the church with the people working on the roof," she said. "I've seen the steeple—I might like to visit."

Questions for reflection and discussion

1. Throughout your journeys, near or far, which steeples have you noticed? Which ones do you take for granted? Which ones cause you to reflect on God's grandeur? On human dreams and ambition?

2. What new meanings do you find in the steeples around you? To what ministries of good news and care are you called as beacons of hope in a world of pain?

4

Centers of Meaning

It was spring in Denver—forsythia, tulips, ornamental crabs all in bloom. A gorgeous day! How could I go inside? But I did. I pulled into the parking lot of Cherry Creek Mall. Lord & Taylor, Saks Fifth Avenue, even Tiffany and Co. beckoned me in, but I realized not many people in Denver could afford to shop in these stores. The store with a jungle motif was fun—and noisy—an "event" shopping destination. The mall has become a gathering place of communal consumerism. I remembered a mall back east, with a stained glass canopy ceiling in the center, promising a cathedral of comfort. We have become more what we accumulate and consume than what we believe.

In chapter 3 we looked up to find steeples of meaning. In this chapter we look around to discover centers of community that are either symbolic or actual. What do they promise? Why are they so inviting? What is their church-like appeal?[1] We may no longer look for "brand names" in churches—Lutheran, Presbyterian, Methodist—but daily we seek our brand names of promised community, for example, Starbucks, the drive-by "shared experience" of Burger King, and Wal-Mart, the latter with "usher-like" greeters and commercials that try to persuade us how much good they do in local communities.

In the center of Cherry Creek Mall was a children's play area with plastic food for recreation. I saw a boy sliding headfirst down a slice of bacon and two little girls playing on the fried eggs. Of course, the waffle was a hit.

I gravitated toward the adult area, complete with overstuffed, living room chairs. People were not interacting, but were together in their solitude. With reading lamps and large bouquets of flowers on the coffee tables, people were reading, resting, and eating. It felt like the lobby of a four-star hotel, and I wanted to linger.

Who comes here? And why? There was nothing in that mall I absolutely needed, but that was not the point. This mall offered a total environment with the promise of meeting all my needs. A full-service community, this was "total church."

The mall appeared accessible. But was it really? Could homeless people sleep here or would they be thrown out? Could a teenager find help for feelings of inadequacy? Who would listen? Could an older adult find anything besides a living room chair to fill one's days with meaning? Was this mall a community?

I had to leave. I wanted to leave. I went to the parking lot, but I wasn't quite ready to drive away yet. I walked the nearby streets with their interesting little shops, allowing myself to get lost in order to see what I would find. At the end of a side street I discovered an inviting gateway: the entrance to Cherry Creek Public School. That same day I had read that school metal detectors do not on their own increase school safety. Cautious not to intrude (I was a stranger), I noted a teacher guiding a group of children putting together a solar system in the walkway with bricks and stones. Other children were quietly playing, teachers calmly chatting. What a wonderfully inviting environment. This public school was a community, a safe place because caring people made it so, accessible to all children, a center of values and meaning and learning.

On my drive away from Cherry Creek I noticed a large sign on the side of a very visible church on University Avenue: "Free Easter Egg Hunt This Saturday." I wondered, "Do some have to pay?" What in the world was this church promising?

All kinds of centers of meaning

Gallerias in Columbus, Atlanta, Baltimore: elegant all. But the most remarkable, I believe, is Lord & Taylor in downtown Philadelphia;

it has an old, elegant dignity about it. There at "vespers," along with lingering shoppers, I heard the powerful, intricate music of the Wanamaker Grand Organ filling the center, seven-story atrium.[2] I sat near the shoe department, on the podium under a large statue of an American eagle. Amid U.S. flags and Christmas trees, mixed together in a holy shrine of American civil religion and secular Christmas, I was enjoying some of the most magnificent music ever composed for pipe organ.

How do we think about church amid these cultural "sanctuaries" of communal meaning? It does not go without notice that many new churches, some nondenominational or trying to be, name themselves "Community of Faith" or "The Gathering Place." Although American people prize their independence, they also hunger for communities with which they can identify and find meaning in a world that feels out of control.

Throughout my journeys I not only observed, but participated in, local communal gatherings. (I went wherever my hosts took me.) I played bingo at a Jewish Community Center in Columbus, Ohio, attended a Lion's Club meeting in Zumbrota, Minnesota, lit candles at a Peace Rally at Rockefeller Center in New York City, stayed all morning at a public auction in Walcott, North Dakota.

My search for centers of community quite naturally took me to central parks. After church on a summer Sunday, I walked around Central Park in Wheaton, Illinois, a comfortable place to be outside with your children. It's just a short stroll to the center of Wheaton, a town on a commuter rail-line to the Chicago Loop, but clearly with its own traditional identity. Wheaton still has a farmer's market, ice cream shops, a good variety of restaurants, and a post office, where people talk to neighbors, unlike "edge cities"[3] of suburbia, which can be residential areas of affluent isolation.

The day before, I had been on Devon Street on the north side of Chicago, a neighborhood where old and new cultures meet: a store where you can buy six kinds of olives; a sari in a bookstore; and

Jewish, Indian, and Russian delicacies and daily necessities. In the Croatian community center I could purchase Islamic religious education material. A visitor can have a real taste of multicultural Chicago today. Just off Devon are the tree-lined side streets, where diverse people meet for human community. But, of course, I could not know, "Do they see each other? Can they learn from one another without being forced to accommodate to the majority culture?"

Today, late Sunday afternoon, I drove down Naperville Road. I stopped in a small mall with its Starbucks, Borders, Pier 1 Imports, and so forth, a place where youth hang out. There was an official "youth room" in this mall. It wasn't open on Sunday. I peeked in the windows; it looked like a church building youth room. I asked a clerk in the store next door (where kids can get their Nikes any day of the week) when the youth room was open. She said she didn't know, but she didn't think very often.

I drove further south on Naperville Road toward the expressway. My eyes turned again to the sign in front of the large business park I had seen from the exit ramp coming into Chicago. "Central Park," it broadcast. "This is a Central Park?" I mused. I decided to delay my departure via Interstate 88 and turned left instead, intent on walking through—as far as I could—this Central Park. The parking lot had only a few cars on Sunday; I found a visitor spot and walked inside this huge complex. I was greeted by an "usher" (guard) with a sign-in sheet. This community of businesses promised a "full-service" life.

Central Park's location is strategic: a clear shot to the Loop (take I-88 to the Eisenhower). It also is positioned on main arteries so that people can live within twenty minutes any direction and have easy access to this business hub. They never have to go into the city at all. (It's just nice to be near all the advantages of Chicago.)

Central Park appeared to offer employees all the advantages of life. Security is provided 24/7. Symbolizing America's love affair with the car and the credit card, this is the corporate headquarters of Budget Rent-a-Car and office center for credit card companies that make all those credit transfers at night, while most of us sleep. And to at least symbolically meet all our needs, Pizza Hut headquarters is here, too. And lots and lots of investment groups. I talked with the guard, a college student who is majoring in marketing, business, and criminal justice (an interesting combination I thought).

A few people were coming and going. A day-care center serves not only employees, but others as well. The athletic club is a big bonus in the business incentive package, no matter what the weather in this Central Park. One can eat in the Central Park Café and pick up necessities in the gift shop. Huge, formal flower arrangements (and not just on Sunday) added color to the chrome and steel.

But of course I couldn't really know what Central Park means to people who are here day after day.[4] I could only wonder.

Questions for reflection and discussion

1. Walk or drive around your community. Go alone, with one friend, or with a group from your congregation. What does community mean where you live? Is it a city block? A residential or commercial neighborhood? A town or township? Dare to "get lost" to see what you find.

2. Where you live, where do people meet? A central park? Do seniors exercise as mall walkers? Do they meet for breakfast in the local café? Where do youth meet? Are there opportunities for cross-generational and multicultural encounters? What do these places promise?

3. As a congregation, what can you learn about human community from such observations? What is countercultural about church steeples and sanctuaries as we gather around Word and Sacrament?

Communities on parade

Who loves a parade? Well, I do. Whether it's the St. Patrick's Day parade in New York City or Indiana, Pennsylvania; the Tulip Festival parade in Pella, Iowa; the Rose Bowl parade in Pasadena, California; or the North Iowa Band Festival parade of my youth, there I am with my camera and notepad. Parades are marvelous places to see communities literally in motion. Such is the annual Memorial Day parade in East Dubuque, Iowa.

The day was cold and promised rain, and I wondered who would come out. But, of course, everyone came, because the people were participants, not merely spectators. A half hour before the scheduled start time, activity centered around the volunteer fire department. Children quickly took the small U.S. flags the firefighters handed out.

People spread out to find good viewing for the three-block long parade route, shorter than the one in Pasadena, but no less exciting. Families and friends shared news, enjoying the gathering time as much as the parade itself. Soon the firefighters gathered to have their picture taken, together with the Roman Catholic priest, their chaplain. I took a picture of the picture-taking. In this highly Roman Catholic community, allegiance to Christian and civil community is blurred. The Knights of Columbus float and marching unit began to form.

The parade began at precisely 9:30 A.M. The East Dubuque VFW, sponsors of the day's events, led off. A car for respected community leaders followed: the Roman priest, the Lutheran and Methodist pastors, and the Dominican sister who serves as parish health minister for the Lutherans and Methodists—and thereby cares for the entire community of two thousand.

Next came the grade school band, a collection of antique cars, the scouts, and then all the rest of the children in town on their decorated bicycles. Then followed the high school marching band, the Amvets, and the floats. Finally the volunteer fire department.

Excitement rose. Their sirens were loud, maybe the loudest I have ever heard at a parade. Or maybe it was because we were so close. Life is close here.

The entire parade took twenty-five minutes, a substantial parade actually. (I've seen smaller.) It all ended quickly and people dispersed. A large number walked up hill onto the bluff over the Mississippi River where pastors and marching units and VFW were waiting in the cemetery. Each year the clergy and sister take turns reading, speaking, and praying. The color guard played, and the Methodist pastor invoked "The Prince of Peace." It would be so easy to glorify the dead of only one nation, one flag. But they didn't. The Lutheran pastor gave the benediction: "Go in peace in the name of the one who died and rose. Go in peace to care for each other and the needs of the world, in this community, in our state, nation, and world."

The lights of Las Vegas

On my way to Las Vegas, driving into Nevada from California, I crossed the border into the small town of Jean, with its two large casinos and a correctional facility. The outside of the casino looked like an old west town, with an ice cream parlor, hardware store, and so forth, but nothing like that existed inside. It was all casino. No windows. People incarcerate themselves here. Casinos promise "the good life," but I felt a deathly sickness.

People in Las Vegas refer to the "gaming industry." I was here to visit a congregation, not the casinos, but one cannot avoid them. Even if you go in for a meal, you have to walk through the main hall, the "sanctuary" around which everything revolves. It is a promised place of community, but most people commune only with the gaming machine.

I did meet real residents of this vacation mecca. I talked at length with a group of community leaders over lunch. Craig travels as a developer. Sue is an investment banker. Marie is an assistant principal in a junior high. John works in public relations in the mayor's office. Mona works for a major casino management firm. Don is a social worker. Kevin is a detective, an investigator in the district attorney's office.

Las Vegas is the newest large city in the country. Three thousand people move here every month. The city may run out of water some day, but that's not on most people's minds, I was told. Building is constant and everywhere, but the city does not feel it has outgrown itself. The surrounding desert is very large.

Fast growth means huge challenges for the city—stress on infrastructure. Mona, who also serves on the board of The United Way, reminded us that people fall through safety nets: The city has the highest high school drop-out rate in the nation and the highest suicide rate for teens.

Marie said, "I see all that every day. High schools have four thousand kids. Some schools have nine or ten portable classrooms out back, only some with air conditioning in 112 degree temperatures. Las Vegas is a training ground for teachers. We hire three thousand new ones each year. You become experienced fast."

Kevin spoke about the impact of gaming on the court system: "We've added an entire new family court structure. People come here and bring their problems with them." People move out here for adventure, opportunity, or a fresh start—to do something different. There's still a sense of "Go west, young man," the frontier mentality. And the intermountain west is largely Mormon with its philosophy of "Be a good citizen and pull yourself up by your bootstraps."

"Yes," John said. "Opportunity, good and bad. If you come here with any weakness, this town will take you down. It makes everything you shouldn't have available."

Craig chimed in, "We have more churches per capita than any place in the United States." People are looking for communities to believe and belong and give meaning to their lives. "And churches pick up a lot of the call for help," said John who serves on the board of St. Jude's for abused and neglected children. Looking at Marie, Don said, "The local school district has done a phenomenal job. We build more schools here in a year than most school districts in the nation have."

More churches per capita? Sure enough! My host, when driving me around the city that afternoon, pointed out many Mormon stake houses, semi-church looking, and the large temple. Later in my motel room, I checked the Yellow Pages: eighty-four different kinds of houses of worship, with one to seventy-four in each category. There were twenty-two each of Lutheran (all grouped under one kind) and United Church of Christ. I found Baptist, Buddhist, and Catholic Byzantine; Unification, Unitarian Universalist, and Unity; Salvation Army, Scientology, Seventh Day Adventist, and SIKH. The longest name was "Harvest Echoes of Faith Effortless Prosperity Grapevine Fellowship." The largest number: nondenominational with seventy-four (and that doesn't include interdenominational or nonsectarian). I didn't visit them all. In Las Vegas, where the sounds of casino sanctuary bells are the slot machines dinging all day and all night and a steeple of the light from the Luxor can be seen from the space shuttle, what can churches with their comparatively small steeples promise?

I visited Community Lutheran Church, with membership of 3,200, and 1,500 worshiping each Sunday. The image I saw was life in the desert symbolized by water—there is a waterfall out front. The prayer chapel has a picture of sea and clouds.

Along with a coffee bar in the huge gathering-place narthex, I saw kiosks of opportunities inviting involvement in many kinds of ministry. I was told, "The freedom to serve is the best kept secret of Christianity; even better than being fed is being able to help feed people. We can't be an entertainment/evangelism show. If the purpose of church is to put on a show, people know they can always find a better one in Las Vegas." Another person added, "We all have sin; it's not just a virus some catch from others. There are many places where people think they find meaning to their lives in Las Vegas. Community of Lutheran is a place people can explore who they are and not be exploited or manipulated, a worship center where the gospel can soak into one's vulnerable places."

Now that's a promise in this lit-up city in the desert.

The church in Cheshire

Cheshire, Connecticut, was first of all a parish. The First Congregational Church was founded in 1724. Fifty years later Cheshire became a town. What happens when a congregation is seen as the center of a community? When the steeple for each is one and the same?

Because this is the "town church," people think they should be married here. When Cheshire third-grade children study history, they start with their town and visit the buildings on the Green; that includes the historical society and the church. The pastor presents the first history session to these children. The town clock is in the church. The town Green belongs to the church. The building is white and statuesque, with a tall steeple, the way "churches are supposed to look," people observe. The steeple is on the Cheshire town seal. A picture of the church hangs in the Chamber of Commerce, is on the cover of the phone book, on the hospital report, and on and on.

Town meetings used to be held in the church fellowship hall. The town's Civil War memorial is on the Green. On one side is Abraham Lincoln. On the other is Admiral Foote, a Cheshire native who was in the Civil War. His grandfather was the second pastor of the church and his father had been governor of Connecticut. How entwined it all was!

"Has it changed?" I asked, when I visited Cheshire. "Yes, it has," I was told by my host, "because of societal mobility—professional people move in and out—and the growing sense of ecumenism in a pluralistic society." In the 1950s this was the "right church" to belong to; now people come only after they have shopped around.

I asked if there were really two churches here. "Yes, the one that is the image of what a church should look like, and the real one, inside the doors where the faith community gathers for worship and education. Today there is a thriving youth ministry and vibrant Bible study for all ages that leads to the full scope of discipleship." A lot is happening here. "I feel the Spirit at work," said the pastor.

"This sanctuary is the most spectacular public space in Cheshire," I was told. No public meetings are held in the sanctuary today, but it remains an apt description of this church. The parish hall, looking more like a town hall, is the place of many community meetings: scouts, Alcoholic Anonymous, the Cheshire Community Band; the African American Seventh Day Adventists; the Iranian Christian group. The Chinese Christian community held its Chinese New Year's celebration here. "This is a far cry," the pastor said, "from the time when, 'If you're not a Congregationalist, keep on going.'"

We walked around the Green and then through the church building. The present sanctuary, the third, is lovely, white and open. We sat for a few minutes in the slave pews. There were still a few slaves owned in Connecticut when this church was built. The Underground Railroad went up the turnpike. In 1960 when the church was remodeled, the congregation decided to keep the slave pews as a reminder of that tragic time in the history of this country.

We climbed the stairs to the top of the tower and saw the workings of the clock. We climbed further up a ladder and out through a trap door into the cupola. We ducked under the bell and saw an aerial view of Sleeping Giant Park a few miles away. I felt the history of the place in which we stood and looked down on the town. This was indeed a significant steeple, and a place of community meeting, in a new way.

Questions for reflection and discussion

1. What pieces of history in your community are carefully maintained? What parts are tempting to discard or forget? How does your history—or newness—shape the present community?

2. How many religious faiths are present in your area? How public are they? Which steeples are seen as more established? Less established? What effect does that have on your membership and mission?

3. When steeple of church and community are one and the same, what are the strengths? The difficulties? When the church as center of meaning is very countercultural, how do people connect to the world? How separate or how much a part of a community should a religious congregation be?

4. What deep hungers do people have as they seek communities of meaning? How does your congregation's message and ministry meet those needs?

5

How Open Are the Doors?

"Open the doors, and see all the people." When we open the doors and look inside a congregation, we see people, gifted by the Spirit, diverse in ability and temperament, age and ethnicity, gender, race and class, joined in a common belief in Jesus Christ. When congregations open the doors and look out, each has a distinct prism through which it views the world.[1] In this chapter and the next we want to open the doors in both directions. We want to see the people and ask how they view themselves. We also want to see the people outside those doors and understand better how the congregation views them and its community as a whole. We also shall consider the difficult issue of closing doors as well as opening them. In this chapter we shall consider "How Open Are the Doors?" and then in chapter 6 explore "How Wide Are the Doors?"

Over the mountain to Shades Valley

Some communities look out at their world, thinking hard about their symbols of meaning and consciously deciding to change their image, slowly perhaps, but markedly. As I drove out of Birmingham, Alabama, I viewed Red Mountain differently than I had just the day before when I had crossed over the mountain ridge to visit Shades Valley Lutheran Church.

I had been introduced to the "New Birmingham" by Gordon, who drove me around his city. The statue of Vulcan, the God of Iron, still stands on Red Mountain, near the southern end of the Appalachians, as a symbol of what Birmingham used to be. Manufacturing had opened the doors of Birmingham, like its English namesake. Birmingham, Alabama, is one hundred twenty years old, post Civil War and therefore not Old South. The industrial revolution fueled the city's fast growth, producing the "Magic City." It was a time of former slaves, former slave owners, and immigrants all working for what were basically northern companies. But now iron ore is low quality and the coal goes to Japan to fuel its steel mills.

The new "Magic City" was beautiful at night. The Civic Center that had been planned to entice the capitol to move from Montgomery (it never did) is now a place of fountains and green space, a place for people to gather. Gordon never mentioned it, because he was painfully aware that I was aware of the image the world had of Birmingham during the Civil Rights Movement of the 1960s. Rather, Gordon wanted me to know that today, "unlike other large cities to the north with high-rises and slums, everyone has a place here."[2] Alabama might be poor, but each person has a piece of ground. Now Birmingham opens its doors through its major medical centers and education. The University of Alabama covers sixty square blocks of downtown.

Shades Valley Lutheran Church opened its doors in 1952. "This relatively new church in a renewing city recently celebrated its fiftieth anniversary," said the parish administrator. Shades Valley intentionally opens its doors every day of the week, providing space for many kinds of groups: seniors on Tuesdays, AA on Wednesdays, Rotary Club on Thursdays. The oldest sponsored scout troop in the city meets here. The church is open to groups from Samford University, just down the road. A counselor—a church member—has her private practice in the building and many community people make use of it. The congregation opened an entire wing to be used as a gathering area. It is the central place for Lutherans in the state to gather for meetings and the host site for Lutheran Ministries of Alabama social services.

"This is Baptist country," I was reminded more than once, so Lutheran churches need to open their doors wide in order to be known. But buildings can't serve on their own. People need to open doors. Congregational members, through their ministries in daily life, are connected to the community in a myriad of ways. And often those ministries lead back to the church, such as a member who works in the medical field inviting the congregation to open its doors to a week-long mental health workshop for people from all over the state.

"Even though there is a lot of mobility in the new Birmingham, there are more people coming in the doors than going away," said one member. Congregation members have supper together most Wednesday evenings during the school year. The Wednesday evening I visited I sat by a teenage boy, Kevin. He told me, "You better listen in confirmation class because down here you have to explain to your friends at school what a Lutheran is." I was impressed that Kevin also invited me to sit with him at the midweek Lenten service that was about to begin. We went into the sanctuary. I was embraced by the joy and warmth of these people, the beautiful organ music, and the bell choir. After a busy day of work, people knew something significant was going to happen as they gathered for worship.

"Andrew" and "Peter" arrived. "Peter" (the manager of the Alabama symphony) was costumed in fishing clothes. He said, "There's not much difference between you and me. I want to control my life; I want to be in charge. But I've found I can't manage my own life." He went on to tell about being a disciple in the young church in New Testament days. "I had been against including those new folks, the Gentiles. . . ." But he had learned. The Christ of the cross had open arms, hands outstretched. So it is at Shades Valley.

Questions for reflection and discussion

1. How wide open are your doors? How is your church building being used? How are people sharing not only the building, but the gospel of Jesus Christ, the redeemer, the teacher, the healer?

2. How do people inside your doors view people in the community, including "new folks"? What views do members hold concerning people diverse in age and ability, race and class?

Keeping doors open in Pennsylvania

I drove through Pennsylvania with its many, many Lutheran churches. Clarkstown (Messiah Lutheran) is easy to see. Lairdsville (St. Mark's Lutheran) is a town you go through and may not even notice. One is in the open valley and the other in a hollow between the ridges. Each church treasures its many years of church doors open for worship. They have been faithful. While mobility and transience is the story of so many congregations I have visited, here things are quite different. Pennsylvania is the state where most people have never lived anywhere else. Even the ones who leave often come back. People found it hard to believe I had driven so far. "Just where are you from again?" Except for a couple of years, this 102-year-old woman had lived in the same house all her life.

The pastor of this two-point parish, her first call, has served here for some time. One might ask how open are the congregation's doors to a pastor who comes from "the outside." "Year four was hard," she said. The pastoral longevity in this 140-year-old congregation had averaged 3.8 years, so people had begun acting as though they expected this pastor also to leave soon. One night at the local community Halloween bonfire, the pastor was getting cold and said off-handedly to a congregation member standing next to her, "I have to go now." "Oh, we've just begun to like you," said the member, assuming the pastor was packing her bags to move on to another congregation.

The word *mission* in many small congregations means "hanging on" and being faithful to their task. That's not easy. When a crisis was brewing and people heard that a church in nearby Williamsport had closed, they began to wonder and worry about their own future. Can closing church doors be catching?

The quilters meet in the church basement every Wednesday. The pastor goes down for some conversation with them and sews a few stitches on every quilt. A few stitches become many—many quilts, many years of faithful ministry.

I drove with the pastor up into the hills to visit a man just released from the hospital. We listened to updates of their blended family. (They had married after each of their spouses had died.) Before we left, we stood and held hands to pray together.

At the fellowship time after a cluster-wide joint Lenten Service, I sat and talked with Dean and Frances and Barb and Gary. Frances and Gary had been at Messiah all their lives. Gary farms, but also works in a factory to support his vocation of farming.

Barbara is a rural mail carrier, diving sixty-four miles and filling 504 boxes every day. She said the Amish children come out to see her; Barbara is their door to the world.

Another evening I attended a meeting of the Ladies Aid. We began with readings from the Epistles, and I brought greetings from the many congregations I had visited, feeling like a living epistle. "Grace to you and peace. We give thanks to God for all of you . . . remembering before God your work of faith and labor of love and steadfastness of hope in our Lord Jesus Christ."[3] We talked about what it might mean to be a stranger and how we might open the doors wide enough to make people really know they are welcome. Frances led and made sure each woman shared. "Helen, you tell about . . ." Ellen, you tell about . . ." She was the inviter. I was the guest. With solid, deep Lutheran roots, they want to keep their doors open for many years to come.

In final preparation for this book, I talked once again with the pastor by phone. The church doors of both congregations are still open. After over nine years of faithful service (the longest a pastor has stayed at St. Mark's), she is preparing for her two final Sundays in Pennsylvania. She said, "St. Mark's has been through some tough times financially. A while ago at a church council meeting I told the congregation, 'We have three choices: 1) We can set a date to celebrate our life and mission and then close; 2) We can continue as we are and go on for few years and eventually close anyway—and that would not be a celebration; or 3) We can look at how we are doing mission in order to open the doors in new ways.'" They have taken the third choice.

"We still are small and finances are still a problem but some neat things are happening. At the annual meeting a few weeks ago, the congregation talked about how we are going to be the church and reach out to community. When it came time to pass the budget, a woman quoted the morning's Old Testament lesson from Isaiah 43, 'Do not fear, for I am with you' (v. 5). The woman said 'I think we need to step out and not be afraid and pass the budget.' Another person said, 'When you put it that way, I second the motion!'

"The very next Sunday I had to tell them I was leaving. After I ended the service with 'Go in peace and serve the Lord,' they sat in utter silence for twenty or thirty seconds. Then I received lots of hugs. The things they have started will keep going. They asked me how they might welcome a new pastor and I said, 'Talk openly. Don't wait until mutters turn into grumbles.' One gift of being here nine years is that the mutters and grumbles are long enough ago that we can chuckle about them now. I am going to miss these people terribly. Norma, I called you during my first year here saying I felt like an alien in a strange land. I remember what you said to me—that I *was* a stranger. There is an itinerancy about pastoral ministry. I knew someday I would need to leave St. Mark's and Messiah, but I didn't want to seek a call when I needed to check the mobility papers box that says, 'Urgent.' Now I can be really open to accepting a call from the Holy Spirit."

As I hung up the phone I remembered Ann Pavia, a woman from long ago who had been a member of our small congregation in a transient, college town. She grew so attached to each person who walked through the doors. She grieved each one's leaving, but I saw her faithfully at the door the next Sunday. I asked her how she could do that year after year and she said, "We worship and grow together in God's love, so I do feel sad. But we can only say to them, 'Peace be with you' and turn to welcome the next stranger coming through the door."

Questions for reflection and discussion

1. How do we say "hello" and "goodbye" in our congregations? How might we?

2. What fears do people in your congregation have about doors closing or doors opening? How do the texts from the Hebrew Scriptures, the Gospels, and the Epistles help us move beyond our hopes, beyond our fears from death into life?

3. How can a congregation claim its own mission and ministry beyond pastoral dependency? How can healthy pastoral leadership foster faithful ministry?

Closing the doors of Hope

Our plane was forty-five minutes late, so I quipped to the man sitting beside me that in that time probably forty-five new houses had been built below us in the greater Phoenix area. So it seemed incongruous to me that Church of Hope was closing. It is incongruous that in a nation so wealthy, by the world's standards, there are such pockets of poverty. "Palms and poverty," the pastor said. The congregation has been here for forty-nine years. "I had hoped they would make it to fifty," she said. The answering machine already announced that the doors would be closing after June 6. The final service would be on Pentecost Sunday, a time to commemorate the birth of the church.

Just a couple of years out of seminary, she recalled that when interviewing for this, her first call, she had been told by the bishop's staff, "We need someone with a lot of energy to turn this church around" and "Money will be no problem." In essence, she had been called to close a dying church.

There are lots of financial and legal things to do as well as giving away worship and education "property." And some people with special memories are just taking things. It's like a family dealing with belongings of a dying loved one. The congregation is in grief, grieving its own death.

At its height, there had been about 250 members, but then white flight began. Now about fifty people worship on a Sunday, a good mixture of Latino, African American, and white; soon they will scatter. Who has power to decide when a neighborhood or church should die?

I remembered a comment from my friend Rich, years before, when we were working in inner city ministry, trying to save a neighborhood from inevitable destruction to make way for encroaching commercial redevelopment. "There can be a lot of good living going on while one is waiting to die." During my visit to dying Hope, I saw good ministry while they were waiting to close.

In the weeks of late Lent, the pastor visits prisoners in Tucson and youth from the congregation and the neighborhood. And there are baptisms and weddings of people never before members of a Lutheran church. Was this not still a mission church? Until just two weeks ago fifty to sixty children came to Hope for day care. "It's so quiet now," said the pastor. The toys remain, but no children. Help for financial support had come . . . but too late.

The building had locks on its doors, not unusual on any church today, even in rural areas. As we walked from room to room through the building we often had to step up or step down. There have been eleven small additions in its forty-nine years (even three different kinds of carpeting in one room). Hope had grown with its needs. How will it be dismantled? Piece by piece, too?

Homeless people live nearby, under the palm trees just off Central. Across the street I saw daily life at a barbershop, a car wash, and some other small business establishments. But the local video store had to pay a manager $20,000 more to come to this area. Sustaining business here is not easy. The warm sun is deceiving. You don't see the gangs and the violence, but they are there. This is prime land . . . or will be again. But redevelopment won't be for the homeless.[4]

Questions for reflection and discussion

1. What is the cost of opening doors and keeping them open to mission in an area that cannot sustain itself financially? What is the cost of closing church doors?

2. Where is the church? What is the church? How can we strengthen partnerships and be a connectional church for ministry in all neighborhoods?

More questions

I ponder many other questions about opening and closing doors. Here are only some:

What about security? How does the need for security affect mission? In visiting an educational institution of the church in an urban area, I was invited to sign the "guest book" at the library, which was actually a way to record who entered the building, what time, and when they left. Can locks and guards and video cameras still be hospitable? Yes, in the midst of those security measures people were friendly and welcoming. In knowing the context, one can be mission-minded and hospitably "open doors" anywhere.

Can one have too many doors? Driving up to a large congregation in a medium-sized city on a Sunday morning I easily found a place to park, but I saw so many doors, it wasn't clear to me which was the main entrance to the sanctuary. I asked a number of people and no one seemed to be able to help me; but each of them seemed to know where to go. I was not noticed as a newcomer. (But I concluded they do open their doors wide; a large class of new members joined the church that day.)[5] At another congregation in another part of the country I talked with leaders who had recognized that same problem. They explained, "With our new addition we had seventeen doors. Which ones were open and when? How could you get in? People were silently divided into outsiders and insiders by whether they knew the secret. We wanted people from the community to truly see this is a hospitable place. We made a welcoming entrance with a glass door, so people could see who and what was inside."

How can one re-open the doors to people who have not been around for a while? In Ohio I was told, "People who identify themselves, 'I used to belong to Good Shepherd,' find it is not easy to come back. They feel others may think, 'You jumped ship; and now you think you can just come back?' But if we are energized and hopeful we can genuinely reach out and be open to the people who left, no matter what their reason."

What if people come in the front door of the church only to go out the back door? A layperson said to me, "Our congregation became so small we had nothing to offer children and youth and so they soon left. When we dwindled from 250 to 25 people at worship, we were advised the pastor should resign and we should close our doors. But we resisted and we've rallied. We've turned things around and are revitalizing ministry and mission."

What if the congregation is being urged to close its doors? In meeting with the council of an open-country congregation in Minnesota, a layperson joked, "We wish the bishop would just tell us what to do . . . so we could be mad at him." But I observed they were already opening their doors in two directions: they were sharing vacation Bible school with two other rural congregations to the west, and they dared to issue an invitation to an urban congregation just a few miles to the east to share in youth and music ministry. "That is the Hispanic edge of the city," they said. This rural congregation is ready to embrace new outreach there. This latest partnership is already proving to be a boost to both congregations.

There are so many creative ways to be the church together. Congregations themselves are designing many models of multiple-point parish and of cooperative work while maintaining separate structures. We need more models of large congregations that truly respect and are open to learning from smaller congregations. All congregations have gifts. We need to work interdependently to open new doors.[6] How are doors opening and closing where you are? What other questions does this raise for you? Who are the people inside and the people outside? How wide open are your doors?

6

How Wide Are the Doors?

How wide are our doors to the world? In this chapter we travel from coast to coast and from border to border of this country, seeing how congregations literally open their doors, reaching out to people who need the liberating power of the gospel. They welcome people in and send people forth to make a difference in the world all week long.

Madison, Wisconsin

We had found our way quite easily around the lakes in the center of Madison, Wisconsin, thereby arriving a little early for the 5:00 Saturday evening service at Lakeview Lutheran. Unlike my other congregational visits, this one was unannounced. My husband, Burton, and I just happened to be in Madison. As we pulled into the parking lot we noticed a quaint, almost miniature church up the hill. Could that be the chapel, where we heard services would be held? (We had naturally assumed the chapel was inside the modern church building.) We looked up the hill and saw two people open the doors and wave their arms wildly for us to come up and enter.

"St. John" was inscribed above the door. This very polished, extremely well-kept building had been started by St. John in downtown Madison long ago. The missionary preacher had traveled by horse and buggy out "to the country" once a week. Now Lakeview is firmly urban, in the middle of the largest Spanish-speaking area of Dane County. Nearby resides a large Hmong community. While as yet few are members of Lakeview, many attend outreach ministries in the building all week long. As we later walked through the large church building, we saw signs to each area: "bathroom," "elevators," and so forth, in English and

Spanish, which said we want you to not only feel welcome but to know your way around inside.

This is a neighborhood of people who work at nearby Oscar Meyer, mental health institutions, and Dane County Human Services next door. Parish health ministries at Lakeview are held each Wednesday evening. A number of people, who are no longer institutionalized but living with mental illness, come and experience the good news of Christ's healing touch. More and more are coming to worship. We quickly saw twenty-first century missionary work, ministries of understanding the world right outside one's doors. We could see that many other people are vigorously waving a "Welcome, come in." The door is wide enough for all.

Dallas, Oregon

Oregonians describe their state as the least churched in the country. They are very independent and proud of it. They are not Washingtonians and certainly not Californians. The pastor at Trinity Lutheran, who has served here in Dallas for seventeen years, grew up in this part of the country and thought it odd when he went to school in the Midwest that people assumed townspeople would go to church on Sunday. He grew up thinking it was a witness to the gospel to simply walk to church while passing people mowing the lawn. Unfortunately that scene is common everywhere now. What remains is the need for intentional witness to the gospel. I found the people of Trinity Lutheran honest in their life struggles and real in holding God at the center of their daily lives.

Dallas, Oregon, is a small city of about thirteen thousand. Old by Oregon standards, it has become a bedroom community for Salem. When the pastor first moved here, he joined the volunteer fire department, not as a chaplain, but to fight fires. He still does. He recommends it as a way to really get to know people, not only the sixty other volunteers, but the whole community.

The weekend we were there, young people were almost constantly in the backyard pool at the home of the pastor's family. He does youth ministry all the time, in a sense. On summer Sunday nights they gather around the pool for Bible study. I was there, too. I talked with Josh for awhile. He told me the young people of Trinity study often, play easily, and work hard. Each summer, right after school lets out, they go on a work trip: building a church on a Native American reservation in Montana, working on a Habitat for Humanity house in Arizona, repairing flood damaged homes in Minnesota and the Dakotas or fire damaged houses in California. Through service, far and wide, they bond as a community of servants beyond their congregation.

We could hear the young people long into the evening from the "chicken coop" next door, where I was staying. Actually it was one of the finer bed and breakfasts of my journeys. Eldon and Lois, members of Trinity, had fashioned a lovely guest house from an old coop and now warmly welcomed guests of the pastor, too. And so it goes as this congregation opens its doors to the world in natural and intentional ways.

The congregation has long opened its doors to Alanon and Alcoholics Anonymous. Some of the leaders in the congregation came through one of those doors. Because of this journey they don't fall into a pattern of dependency. You don't hear the laity saying, "Pastor you should do something about . . ."

People use church space all week, sometimes three groups a night. There are the scouts, of course. A local artist comes in to work with children, and there is a writing group for adults. "Not only is this good stewardship of the building," said the pastor, "but churches today are less and less valued by a municipality unless they are seen as serving the community." The size of the congregation has doubled since this pastor came. People who live in the world all week know they are hungry for God's grace. "People don't do lines in society anymore," said the pastor. "For communion we all gather around the altar," which has fishnet paraments.

How does the church open its doors wide to people in this era? The pastor responded, "Pantheism describes our culture. In this world of many gods, the Lutheran church is in a unique position. When you start talking Lutheran theology of cross and resurrection to people between the ages of twenty and thirty, they get excited. It's like Paul standing in front of the Areopagus, saying, 'Athenians, I see how extremely religious you are in every way.' And then, looking carefully at all the objects of their worship he found an inscription to an 'unknown' God (Acts 17:22ff). Our goal is opening wide the doors to these young adults who are searching and may not even know it. They don't want something phony. It is saying: 'Let me tell you about this God.'" In addition to preparing young men and women for ministries in their own daily lives, this congregation has sent a number of students to seminary.

Trinity reaches out to older people, too. A Friday morning group is studying—of all things—the Book of Numbers. "It's a great book for transition to a new place," the pastor said. People worry about their adult children. We need to reach out to each other's grown-up children, helping them once again become part of the gospel story.

The pastor here is well-loved and trusted. "It's important, over the years," he said, "to keep expectations high."

Questions for reflection and discussion

1. How do we continue to warmly, even "wildly," wave in people through open doors?

2. As new people come through the doors of our congregation, how can we address possible anxieties of long time members? How do we assure them that they and their gifts are still needed? How do we foster deep relationships between old and new?

3. As community outreach ministries deeply touch people's lives (AA, Alanon, and so forth), how can those changed lives help change congregations?

Old Tappan, New Jersey

We met in the church lounge because it was a dark, rainy day. Prince of Peace in Old Tappan is in northern Bergen County, one of the wealthiest areas in New Jersey. This community is not suburban—too established for that. This is the Jersey side of metropolitan New York City. People are oriented to and commute to the city. Old Tappan has winding streets, beautiful old homes, the type of location to which most Americans, while climbing the economic and social ladder, aspire to move. In contrast, Hackensack, the county seat, has homeless people.

Some residents of Old Tappan trace their roots back to the Revolutionary War—old money. But there is new money here, too. As land prices rise even higher, some people are moving in, tearing down the old smaller homes to build a "McMansion."[1] Property taxes are high. Churches can be viewed as a liability since they take expensive land off the tax roles. In fact the door to opening new churches is virtually closed because zoning requires three-and-one-half acres of property that costs half a million dollars an acre (and going up), even before you start to build.

Old Tappan is politically conservative. Women's clubs and the Junior League flourish. Civil gatherings request a pastor to lead them in prayer. On Memorial Day clergy march in the parade, but this civil religion has a deist quality to it. More central to people's lives is belonging to the country club—or tennis and racquetball clubs for those to whom the country club's doors are closed. How does one open church doors here?

Episcopalians are quietly strong, but it is the Dutch Reformed who have long been the establishment religion. The Jewish population is substantial. Today there are many people of Korean descent here; the Korean Presbyterian in Old Tappan is a mega, regional church. Lutherans are low on the social scale.

Prince of Peace Lutheran focuses on worship, learning, and service—acts of love. One might be surprised to discover homeless single adults housed in the church building Monday nights in November and December, bused here from other places in Bergen County. This ministry has continued for over thirteen years as part of the Interreligious Fellowship. Likewise, Prince of Peace opens its doors wide to residents of a psychiatric center in Rockland County, New York, for worship and activities. There is some concern that the new people moving "up" to Old Tappan might be resistant to sharing their new zip code with such guests. But Prince of Peace members are committed to such hospitality. Hertha, a deaconess and retired social worker, has done much to promote an ethos of love and community at Prince of Peace.

This congregation knows that Old Tappan needs God's mercy, too, to combat the spiritual poverty that wealth can produce. The pastor cited Luke where the rich man, whom God calls a fool, tears down storehouses to build even bigger ones.[2] "Wealth has power for great good, but riches also can create chaos in people's lives," the pastor said. (This pastor had worked for a large accounting firm before attending seminary and understands the rat race.) The challenge is to reach out with the gospel to help people see Christ as the center of their powerful, even prestigious lives. In addition to Bible study, they use *Connections: Faith and Life*,[3] based on *Luther's Large Catechism*, to help people be grounded in their faith and live out their calling to serve Christ, whatever their vocation in the world.

While completing the manuscript for this book, my travels took me once again to Old Tappan. It was Palm Sunday. I was welcomed into the sanctuary in the round not just by one or two people, but by person after person. They saw me. They clearly see each other. They see the cross suspended over the altar and can look beyond the cross through the skylight into the world. A woman who was running for school board asked support of the congregation. The congregation will be starting a preschool in the fall. An interracial, interfaith family has begun to attend church regularly. The pastor invited all children to a mini-retreat on Good Friday, a hands-on education experience to understand the stories and meaning of Holy Week. The prayers to the Prince of Peace were for peace in the whole world. I experienced the warmth, joy, challenge, and commitment of the people of Prince of Peace Lutheran who continuously ask what it means to be faithful to the gospel in a complex world that as yet has found no peace.

Questions for reflection and discussion

1. How does the church underestimate itself in regard to the influence it can have in the world? What opportunities do the people in your congregation have in daily life to reach people with the love of Christ?

2. How can your church enrich its educational ministry to equip people for ministry inside and beyond the doors of the congregation?

Dickinson, Texas

From the air I could see the tall, boxy buildings of Houston. I could also see Galveston Bay and the steeples of Texas City oil refineries. Somewhere in between was Dickinson. Upon landing I discovered this is bayou country, so the earth is clay. January had been wet and cold and the water table is only a foot or so down. My feet felt the squishy bog.

The Houston-Texas City-Galveston area is growing by leaps and bounds. Dickinson is becoming a bedroom community for the whole area.[4] So far, Dickinson has kept its flavor. It was not hard to find the congregation, although in this region many Lutheran congregations identify themselves: "Go to a Baptist church and then look next door." Yes, the Baptists had built their large church right up to the street; that hides the view of Faith Lutheran next door.

Inside Faith Lutheran Church I felt the warmth. Faith is solidly Lutheran. What message do people hear? The group of eighteen people who gathered at a Sunday noon meal told me:

"We who grew up in other churches experienced religion as constrictive, restrictive, and oppressive. At Faith Lutheran we hear love, grace, and forgiveness again and again and again."

"I heard that you had to be good or God would punish you, so I pretended a lot and separated church from daily life. When I heard that God loved me unconditionally, I could be honest, confess sins, and receive forgiveness."

"The body of Christ has a body here."

"Adult Sunday school keeps me here."

"This is an educating church. I can be open about my questions."

"People come out of the woodwork when there is a need."

"People sustain each other here. I see the gospel at work."

"There's a lot of tradition. And a lot of loving your neighbor, too."

And straightforward talk. I asked if I was keeping them too long. A man said, "If we get tired, we'll get up and leave." The people didn't leave for two hours.

Two days earlier I had had lunch with community leaders in a local restaurant with distinctly Spanish decor: the head of the volunteer fire department, the mayor, and the city planner (Roman Catholic, Methodist, and Baptist). "We need all of the churches. They have key roles in providing discussion and assessment of need, such as for a senior housing center," said the city planner. "The only place the whole town really comes together is at the Friday night football game." Those are community events all over Texas. They still have student led prayers at the games.

The boom growth is moving south, with new subdivisions going up. "We'll grow from twenty thousand to forty thousand in the next fifteen years. We don't have many snowbirds here," said the mayor. The fire chief said, "People move to Dickinson away from Houston, and far enough away from the oil refineries so they are outside the blast zone. (They are mindful of the Texas City explosion fifty years ago and the Galveston Hurricane of one hundred years ago, killing thousands.) Developers are building lakes where there weren't any ("Dig a hole and you'll find one"). "We need to work on our infrastructure," said the city planner. "We're a late bloomer, but we'll be ready for the future."

The mayor visits various churches. He said, "The minister's primary function is spiritual welfare, but they also have to care for the total person and that total person lives in the community. Ministers can have an impact on the lives of people in the community." It was clear to me that churches are welcome to open their doors of influence wide here.

Faith Lutheran has a clear, strong mission statement. Its Web site provides direct answers to the questions "What is a Christian?" and "What is a Lutheran?" It says, "We are a congregation of the Evangelical Lutheran Church in America, located in Dickinson, Texas. . . ." Having their doors open to the broader church body sustains them for their mission in Dickinson, Texas.

Faith's lead pastor has served here twenty-three years. Another pastor, a meteorological engineer in Houston, is called to a nonstipendiary pastoral ministry at Faith. I also met a visitation pastor. This strong Lutheran leadership told me, "We don't need to out-Baptist the Baptists. Lutherans have a strong center, deep commitments, and open questions. We need to hold to that sacred center of justification by grace through faith in Jesus Christ."

One pastor went on, "I think the style of evangelical boom . . . where people get a hot praise band and assume people will simply come, is kind of petering out. Maybe in trying to open the doors that way we have been trying to be what we are not; we create a boom and bust environment. Rather we need to offer real hospitality that helps people get through the front door and connects them with community. 'Learn the faith, serve, and love is our goal.'"

He continued, "We send mailings to new residents and extend more invitations at special seasons of the church year. We direct things, such as art events, outward not just inward. We have a significant early childhood learning center. We know we have a mission to reach out to people burned out by evangelicalism that runs merely on fervor." Faith Lutheran Church understands its evangelical witness of grace and lives it.

Questions for reflection and discussion

1. How can keeping a congregation's doors open to the broader church help sustain it in its mission?

2. Ask people in your congregation what grace means in their lives. Ask some community leaders what keeping the church doors wide open means to them.

How wide?

Just how wide open are the doors? That question is a metaphor, of course. I began this chapter with a vignette from Madison; I close it with a snapshot from Montana. You can see far and wide up here; Montana is Big Sky country. Dave, a former state senator, now radio broadcaster, showed me around. He described Montana as "a little town with very long streets."

On Sunday, from the sanctuary of King of Glory Lutheran Church, Billings, Montana, I looked out into the world through the clear glass windows: the Rimrocks, Beartooth Mountains. "The earth God created is infinitely superior to any building we could create, so we have no artificial barriers between faith and life," said the pastor.

"How wide?" may ask how broadly one is able to connect with people. In Montana one is likely to know someone in every part of the state . . . and to be known. Dave told me the story of a young man who was driving home one night. It was getting very late. He knew his parents would worry about him, so he decided to stay overnight in Helena. He thought about any names of people he knew there and made a call to a residence in the phone book—the governor's house. He did find a bed there that night!

"How wide?" means paying attention to people's perspective and points of reference. People come to Montana to "make it" and many don't, because it's rugged life. You can see the big sky because no tall buildings get in the way. They don't feel fenced in. People look either west to Seattle or east to Minneapolis and St. Paul. In some ways people relate more directly to Calgary, Alberta. King of Glory, now twenty years old with seven hundred members, continues to grow rapidly. But attrition is high, too, because people who come to work for Conoco and Exxon also transfer out. How does one continue to open the doors wide when the doors seem to be revolving doors?

Each congregation has its own challenge. I have found that mission and ministry are not easy anywhere, just differently difficult. "There is a general reluctance here to define ourselves over and against others," a layperson told me. "Distinctiveness is not that important. Our doors are wide open to all." Another said, "There is a saving grace at King of Glory [even though people are a little uncomfortable with that triumphalist sounding name]. We keep first things first: like grace and faith."

Each place is a unique place. One needs to learn to cherish the vista and the vision, the people and their gifts. So it was in Montana. When people there proudly told me they even have their own cereal—"It's not Cream of Wheat" out here; it's "Cream of the West"—I wondered if they were putting me on. But just before I left, the pastor came by to bring me a box. Sure enough: Cream of the West!

7

See the People

We look around church and see people. But our view is limited. We see people in the pews every week but may have no idea what they do all week in their ministries in daily life. We may look through a nostalgic lens seeing only what used to be, "when the pews were full," thereby unable to fully appreciate the gifts of the present or the promise of the future. These two final chapters, "See the People" and "Cherish the People" focus on how opening the doors can help us see each other more clearly and to envision people who may not yet be part of our faith community.

Questions for reflection and discussion

1. As you look around at the people in your congregation, who do you see? What do they have in common? What is the range of diversity?

2. As you look around in the community, who do you see? How might you broaden your vision?

Remember your thoughts as you read these four stories.

Pickerel Lake Township

The directions were clear: From Interstate 35, turn left on 13, then right on 69, then left on 17, then right on 14, and then left on the gravel road. Upon arrival, my first impression was not how remote this area is, but how beautiful. Concordia Pickerel Lake Lutheran, Albert Lea, Minnesota, has 340 baptized members. Because I arrived on a Friday morning, I did not see the worshiping community, but rather the well-tended and frequently visited cemetery, a visual reminder of the communion of saints.

The pastor has served here six years, and she is trusted. She said that she and her family might stay here many more years: "The culture dictates you must 'move up the ladder.' We don't have to! It is joyful to be in a church where you know the people intimately and where they want the very best for their pastor." I realize this is not always the case.[1]

"We're in the midst of a baby boom," she said. "Nine baptisms since September." Some new young families are deciding to live in the country or to drive out from the nearby city to be part of this faith community, contrary to demographic predictions about the rural upper Midwest.

To see the people at Concordia one must understand deep and broad root systems of large extended families. I met the church council president Friday noon. He mentioned his mother, who is, naturally, a member of Concordia. I chatted with her on Sunday. She was going to visit her mother at the nursing home that afternoon. And generations before that are buried in the churchyard. People know each other's parents and grandparents, as rare a luxury in today's culture as a baby boom at a country church. And yes, when someone is hurt in a farm accident one quickly sees fifteen combines coming up the road to bring the harvest in.

Throughout my visits, the most common building project I have seen I saw here, too: expanding the narthex for people to talk in all kinds of weather and providing accessibility.[2] In anticipation of welcoming people not yet visible, the congregation shortened benches in the middle of the sanctuary to accommodate wheelchairs. They didn't want seated people in the back where they couldn't see. This turned out to make the sign of the cross in the center of communal worship. The space was quickly used for wedding guests. The very first was a child in a wheelchair.

Concordia has looked around and seen suffering people, some with obvious need, others with hidden pain. They, as many other congregations, have re-established the historic liturgical practice of healing services. The pastor said, "We have them at various times during the church year, when it fits the texts, which is not difficult since so much of Jesus's ministry was about healing. Not after the service, but within the service for everyone. You would be surprised all those who come up for laying on of hands, young as well as old."

Concordia is "not waiting until we are gasping for breath and life." "We can't wait until people find us. We are exploring." They reach out to people who are not even here yet, and to other congregations for collaborative ministry opportunities, so that, together, they might see people and serve.[3]

From Pickerel Lake to Pasadena

From Pickerel Lake, Minnesota, to Pasadena, California, change is a challenge everywhere. At Messiah, near downtown Pasadena, I found people with eyes wide open to see new people precisely because of their long, Lutheran heritage.

Messiah's founding Lutherans in 1912 were maids, gardeners, all Swedish immigrants. For its first twenty-five years the church was bilingual. Membership peaked in the 1960s. Then the neighborhood (one-half mile in each direction) changed and members moved away. But Messiah integrated and soon had strong African American leadership families. By the mid-1970s Messiah had developed a very community-oriented ministry, including outreach through a small school and a Head Start program.

But that's not the end of the story. In the late 1970s, the neighborhood changed again. Latinos came, Mexican Americans and refugees from Central America. Messiah, remembering its own immigrant heritage, once again readjusted its vision to see new needs. They offered English classes. The faithful at Messiah Lutheran try to really see the people, as did the Messiah, and to get to know them. About a year later, they began weekly Eucharist in Spanish.

The pastor, at the time of my visit, had a Scandinavian name and had learned Spanish. As we walked the neighborhood together, he spoke fluently with people we met. Bungalows lined quiet residential streets. He pointed out what I did not see: second little houses in the courtyards behind with as many as ten people, recently arrived, joining extended families. There may be over four hundred people on one block. Many are very poor; Pasadena stores within walking distance are expensive.

When it started to rain heavily (yes, it does rain in sunny southern California), we headed back to church. There I saw encircling the sanctuary wonderful modern paintings depicting the Stations of the Cross. An artist, a member and the son-in law of a second-generation Swedish American member, wanted to do something for Messiah. Many Latino Christians believe it is disrespectful for a church to have bare walls. Long-time Lutherans like them as well.

Being committed to multicultural, bilingual ministry is a first step. Sustaining it over the years is challenging and can at times be discouraging. Since my visit, the Latino membership has grown slowly. Even though the English-speaking membership grew smaller, they faithfully supported mission outreach. The evangelism question: "What is God calling us to do in this time and place?"

There have been various partnerships of Anglo and Latino pastoral leadership in recent years. Both are needed. Recently I spoke with one. "For example," she said, "as a new Anglo pastor, while I was teaching thirteen first Communion children who could speak English, their mothers sat in the back. The Hispanic pastor said he would meet with the mothers, who knew little English."

Messiah now uses its facilities for a social service outreach, including "Mother's Club" for women and children, various Alcoholics Anonymous and Narcotics Anonymous groups in Spanish, English as a second language classes, Saturday morning tutoring classes for neighborhood children, and the area Head Start kitchen. The goal: to reach out in the name of Christ with love to all people who live in the neighborhood and to invite people to become part of the ministry to serve people in their need."

It takes consistent support from the broader church to sustain mission through the ups and downs of growth and decline. I asked, "Today, do you have one congregation or two?" I was told, "We have one congregation, one budget, one church council, half Anglo and half Latino. We have a bell choir with Latino, Anglo, and African American people playing together. Our long-term commitment to multicultural ministry means moving beyond excitement about the number of new people we are reaching. We go deeper and deeper, working through crises, facing the subtleties of racism, classism, sexism, and the realities of just how differently we function."

The pastor went on, "This church has been faithful for so many years. I believe God wants the Lutheran church here to see all the people, the problems, and the possibilities. The birthing of a healthy multicultural church comes from transformational ministry."[4] This means understanding forgiveness at a deep level, so we can thrive. "These are precious people." I could feel her love. "We want to be part of the birthing pains of God opening up our whole church body."

I thought, "In the birthing process one cannot stop in the midst of the labor pains." To see all the people is not simply for a church to move from serving one solitary racial or ethnic group to serving another solitary group, but to be together, a rarity in our culture. How can we learn not only to see each other but to love each other at this deepest level?

Living Lord in Lake St. Louis

I left north central Iowa at dawn because I would be driving almost the full length of the Avenue of the Saints (St. Paul to St. Louis) that day. After crossing the river into Missouri, the highway became narrower; large, lovely tree limbs shaded the road. I was met with a barrage of fireworks sales. One store offered fireworks, hand crafts, and hand-crafted fireworks.

It was flooding season this April; the fields on either side of the road would not be planted soon. The yellow clay and bluffs reminded me I was very close to the Mississippi, my river upstream. But this was downriver. Once we got to Hannibal and beyond, the signs promised St. Louis.

I drove in from the west of the city: Lake St. Louis. Living Lord congregation began in 1981 as a mission. It now has over twelve hundred members ("disciples"). The suburb beyond the suburbs expanded so quickly that the congregation outgrew its relatively new building, which I had visited three years earlier. In March they broke ground for a new building, on the other side of the lake, and they were in by Christmas. You build fast in the suburbs. The school district has to build two new schools a year.[5] Living Lord is considering how, in partnership with a coalition of Lutheran churches, they might plant a new church further west. They envision people who are not yet here, but are coming.

If in Pasadena people are hidden behind crowded bungalows, here, hidden behind the doors of expensive homes, are the incongruities of people's lives. Beyond the beautiful doors may be illness, personal struggles, or serious money problems. Meanwhile, five hundred yards southeast of Lake St. Louis, MasterCard built its new international headquarters employing four thousand people. Culturally, we are compelled to live on credit. And "convenience" is the byword. People are expected to live the ideal life around the lake, conveniently.

In the midst of a culture pursuit of luxury leisure, is Living Lord an anchor for faith in Lake St. Louis? I listened to congregation members who had gathered for a Saturday noon lunch:

"Life often feels crazy, out of control. The gospel is here no matter how crazy life becomes."

"We hear a gospel of unconditional love, acceptance no matter who you are; you don't have to look like 'somebody.'"

"Remember the purpose in our growing: to speak the gospel. To tell people, 'You are loved.' People—all people—need to hear that."

"In the suburbs, where people drive everywhere, we need to continue to create a faith community. You can't create community through a windshield."

"Living Lord is a good name for us. Living! And Jesus Christ as Lord, no other."

The conversation deepened further:

"This is a more transient place than may appear. Corporate America moves people around a lot."

"A corporate church brings the danger of people giving money but not themselves. People need to know that they are needed."

"People reach out and bring people in, and then others reach out. Evangelism is catchy."

How do these people see their neighbors of other faiths? At education hour on Sunday I entered an adult forum room, already packed. The guest was a local Jewish woman, a schoolteacher, whom one of the pastors had met while working on ecumenical and interfaith issues in the community. Together they organized the first "Stop the Hate" rally in the area, which then led to a coalition.

Sunday morning's adult forum was part presentation, part discussion, and part debate. There is clearly much diversity among Lutherans on interfaith relations. Some were curious about Judaism today and asked questions. A couple brought up the need to evangelize Jews to which a woman replied, "We are saved through Christ; I'm going to leave it up to God how others are saved." A man said, "The Christian religion is being hijacked by fundamentalists; they could suck me into hating Arabs." Such lively adult forums need good resources and wise leaders to sustain a trustworthy learning environment. The conversation continued through the congregation all week long.

Late Sunday afternoon, while my gracious host, Vonne, was out, I was left to myself in her beautiful home. I went down by the dock to listen to the water gently lap the shore. A boat stopped off shore and people called out, "Would you like a ride?" I couldn't see who they were, but I trusted they had recognized me. So I said, "Yes." It was Mandy and husband, Randy, from church, their son Kyle, and his friend. They said, "We wondered whose legs those were on Vonne's dock." We had a forty-five-minute conversation. I had yet another view of people: from lake to shore. They pointed out that older homes look small compared to those being built now. They talked about pressure on kids in an affluent society. "Water skiing here for our youth is very competitive."

I saw the people through their eyes. With counterculture commitments, people gather around Living Lord with a heart to serve. The congregation and pastors of Lutheran congregations here, and everywhere, are politically diverse. Yet, when they see a real person with a human need, they respond as one, quickly and generously, to meet that need. They know they must be deeply grounded in scripture with a willingness to listen and to really see the people amid affluent surroundings.

Church

Idaho Springs, Colorado, on the eastern slopes of the Rocky Mountains, was a mining town, gold and silver mainly. It still is, but mining is sporadic now and the economy goes up and down. People drive into Denver to work. Others make their living off the ski trade. But for the most part, people pass by on their way to somewhere else—higher slopes. I had sometimes passed by, too, but this time I wanted to stop and look around. Idaho Springs has two streets with homes and a few shops . . . and a few other houses further up the slope. There are some wealthy people as well as down-and-outers, independent people with independent reasons for being here. On the side of the Lutheran church building is a large sign, very visible from the road, which says "Church." The story goes they couldn't reach higher to put "Zion" above.

This congregation has had thirty-six pastors in its 108 years. They have struggled. At times they worshiped every other Sunday in the basement because they couldn't afford to heat the sanctuary. They have a sense of loyalty to the church, but commitment to ministry is a challenge. Idaho Springs is full of people who are unchurched; many want to be left on their own. But in the midst of such rugged individualism, somehow, through God's grace, "Church" is still here.

During my visit Zion was being served by an interim pastor. She said, "The people here have good hearts." Late afternoon we stopped by Loraine Kutch's house at the end of the lower road. She's in her late seventies. When people needed food from Kutch's grocery, but had no money, she and her husband often would carry folks on the books. Who knows if they ever paid. The Kutches literally fed the town when the economy was down.

About 5:30 P.M., while the pastor got ready for mid-week Bible class and Lenten worship, I went for a walk. I wanted to explore. A teenager asked me which way I was going so that he could "come find me if I didn't come back." He suggested walking east, down by Clear Creek. I did. I sat on the rocks, hearing "surround sound" provided by water rushing through the creek bed. Home fountains are popular these days, but this was the real thing. I sat there for a half hour.

When I returned I met Jeff, a handsome young adult with cerebral palsy, climbing down the stairs. His mother had put his walker at the bottom. It took him time, but he made it himself.

All sorts of people were arriving, bringing kettles of soup, sandwiches, and corn bread into the cozy fellowship hall. The food was wonderful. So were the people.

I discovered Jeff and his family had recently become members of Zion. Karen is building a house with a geodesic dome. She has long, gray hair and plays the sax. Daryle is a retired miner. A couple had moved here from Minnesota. Another woman, self-professed "born again," told me she had tried every church in town before coming to Zion. She plants "crack gardens" (seeds in the cracks in the side-walks). Some people say what come up are weeds, but she believes such plants are there on purpose.

After we ate, the youth took over a corner of the fellowship hall with their leader for their fourth session on the Book of Jonah. I had been told that in the high school the largest group of students are atheists, the next in size, agnostics, and then pagans.

We as adults gathered around the big, red-checkered tablecloth to have our discussion on Jonah with the pastor. It was a jovial forty-minute study. People listened to each other.[6]

Daryle, paraphrasing God, began: "Hey look, Jack, I made this plant and I can take it away. You want to die? Tough! When you grow faint you must be trying to do it your own way."

A woman said, "We haven't come very far, have we? By color or culture, we still are resistant to inclusion."

Karen probed a deeper question, "Did God use Jonah for the Ninevites or the Ninevites for Jonah and for us?" Maybe Jonah thought—and we think—the Ninevites will just fall back again."

A person at the end of the table said, "Maybe God was saying that Jonah had a task now of tending the Ninevites." How do we tend the stranger?

The discussion could have gone on, but it was time for worship. The twenty-five of us climbed narrow stairs to the sanctuary. The pastor asked if someone would read Psalm 102 so we could just lis-ten to the words without having to pay attention to our own read-ing. A young person volunteered. "Hear my prayer, O Lord; let my cry come to you. . . . Long ago you laid the foundation of the earth, and the heavens are the work of your hands."[7] It was very moving in the dimly lit church on the mountain slope with dark evergreens around. We prayed *Lutheran Book of Worship* Responsive Prayer 2 and then sang.

Four years later: According to the answering machine, Zion Lutheran still has Wednesday evening prayer service. Sunday morning service is at 10:30 with Sunday school before. But repeated calls resulted only in the message. With a call to the synod office I was able to get in touch with the most recent pastor who had been serving half time. The congregation had recently voted to let her go because they didn't have funds to pay her anymore. They will now use supply pastors.

I could tell from her voice how much she loved the people. I could see them: Yes, Daryle is still there. Loraine Kutch's husband died. She just turned eighty. Karen is still working on her geodesic dome home. Jeff's brother is serving in Iraq.

The recently released pastor went on: "You should see the stained glass windows now! The congregation worked on them for twenty years. An artist taught people to cut glass from the old windows to fashion the new. Together we selected hymns that reflect each season of the church year. We just finished two! Epiphany: 'Brightest and Best of the Stars of the Morning' and Easter: 'Jesus Christ Is Risen Today.'[8]

"I baptized a whole family on my next to the last Sunday with them," she said. With windows reflecting the Lutheran heritage and doors open, "Why has this church survived into its 108th year?" she questioned aloud. "God must have a purpose for this church to be here."

Questions for reflection and discussion

1. How can we begin to see "hidden" people?

2. How can we have vision to see people who are not yet here?

3. How can congregations truly be accessible to all people, diverse in age, ability, gender, language, race, and economic and educational class, becoming truly multicultural?

4. How has God sustained your congregation through the years? How can we as congregations support each other through the struggles?

8

Cherish the People

As we look around and consider our location and identity, as we ponder the steeples of influence in a world seeking meaning, as we look at the people inside our congregations and in the communities beyond, we see the challenge that awaits us. We could be overwhelmed and want to close the doors once again. After all, to open the doors wide may be to reach beyond our means physically and financially. At that very moment when we feel unqualified for the task or depleted of energy, our merciful God reaches out to embrace us once again, and to remind us who and whose we are. God cherishes us! In God's grace we have strength and love to cherish the people among whom we are blessed to serve.

Again and again I have talked with pastors, congregation members, and community leaders who doubt they are fit for the task or who fear the future. A pastor called and said, "Norma, there was a terrible fire last night and the church is gone. I'm not prepared to lead these people through this." But, of course, she was and she did! She simply needed to hear once again that God had prepared her and would lead her as she leads God's people.

And countless times I have listened to people who are frustrated, angry, hurt, cynical . . . just plain tired to the bone from conflict in the congregation. There are no quick ways to glue together that which has been torn apart. All of us—all of us—have participated in breaking apart the body of Christ. But that Christ, who knew betrayal and who was abandoned on the cross, is alive and has chosen us to be his risen body in the world, mending and healing, seeking justice, and working for peace.[1] We who have been cherished by a creating, forgiving, empowering God, rise each morning to remember our baptism so that we might cherish the people God has created.

Highlands Ranch

"Imitate the wheat. Unless it falls into the ground, it remains alone," said the seasoned pastor who has served at Lutheran Church of the Holy Spirit for fourteen years. The Spirit has indeed been at work through him in his congregation and beyond. We are never and can never remain alone. On the way to the restaurant to join his wife, also a pastor,[2] for lunch after their respective Sunday morning services, he took me by the cemetery where crosses marked a memorial to the people who died at Columbine.[3] The first anniversary would fall on Maundy Thursday. Holy Spirit is in Denver, not the southern suburbs, so his ministry was caring for the caregivers. As dean of his conference of twenty-two congregations, in the weeks following the tragedy he took each pastor to lunch to ask how they were doing. Pastors who cherish the people often have no one to listen to them. The pastor was still somber, "How do you mourn? How long is the season for grieving?" And how are all of us in all of our grief joined together as we walk through Holy Week as a global church? There is so much tragedy, so much grief everyday around the world. The Holy Spirit embraces us with Christ's love to cherish the people way beyond our own congregations.

I spent the next day with the pastor of Christ Lutheran in Highlands Ranch, very near Columbine High School, and very directly affected by that tragedy. The congregation and Highlands Ranch are both young and growing fast. Finding enough time and space are stress points. Nobody was born in Highlands Ranch, so people who move to this suburb bring their hopes, dreams, and different traditions with them. The congregation holds a new member class every other month with about sixty people in it; that is church growth of about one member a day: sixteen hundred baptized.

The pastor brings grace and administrative attentiveness to his leadership role. He has an infectious laugh. It was so good to see him. I sat in on the morning meeting of the large congregational staff where I witnessed that each leader is respected and valued.

Then we went out to lunch. (The pastor had redefined a long-scheduled business luncheon appointment so we could talk about ministry.) Our host was a self-described, "divorced, remarried, always Lutheran, stock broker, and financial salesman." He said, "There are no funeral homes, hospitals, or nursing homes in Highlands Ranch. People are supposed to move here and live forever. It's part of the suburban myth." With a twinkle in his eye, he added, "We know that statistically Lutherans invite a person to church every twenty-seven years, but people come here from other traditions so they don't know they should wait that long to invite someone." More seriously: "People are searching. People can speak about church because everyone in the area is new and asking for information. It's not so much flyers at the door as friends reaching out and bringing new friends and neighbors."

We talked about people's values and vision. He went on, "In understanding people here, one must understand the difference between wealth and affluence. If you have wealth you have assets. Affluent people may have a good income, but live with mortgages and debt. It's capitalism gone wild!" I could see this man takes his Lutheran Christian faith very seriously: "Through life our values change. It's all about self-actualization. First me-me-me. Then my family, me-me-me. Then my community, me-me-me. Finally you must ask, 'What do I want all this stuff for?'" To cherish people with the word of God here may seem challenging, but no less so than anywhere in the United States among our many competing steeples of meaning.

After lunch, the pastor and I went to see Columbine High School. In that time of tragedy, the people of Christ Lutheran surrounded one another in the congregation and the community with prayer and care. As weeks went on: more grief, and more prayer, preaching, nurture on the sacraments, study of the Word, counseling. Time passes but, "We know we will never be the same," said the pastor.

The number of deaths by guns in the United States makes it by far the most dangerous large country in the world. I was told that schools simply putting in locks, metal detectors, and armed guards actually can make children feel less safe. Neither does increasing the number of prisons make people feel more safe. People living in community have to create an atmosphere of trust. I saw in the ministry of Christ Lutheran faithful ministry that calls people together to face the many layers of shock, suffering, grief, guilt, blame, notoriety, the press, and the personal and familial aftershocks. Together we need to face the issues of violence in this culture and do something about it. That is how we love and cherish all God's people.

Four years later: I talked with the same pastor again recently. The rate of growth at Christ Lutheran continues. Now there are two thousand baptized members. "But statistically we lose 'one-half' a member a day because of suburb mobility," he said. And with that many people, participation can flatten out. He told me they are determined to emphasize: "The primary role of Highlands Ranch's large staff is to equip and strengthen the ministry of all the baptized."[4] To cherish the people is to cherish their gifts to undergird multiple ministries and to reach out. People want to participate in ministry directly.

With four worship services and no room to expand (and carrying a two-million dollar debt), they are considering starting a second campus near Interstate 25, south toward Castle Rock. The pastor said, "Like the church at Philippi, one congregation in multiple places. Denver continues to build south and Colorado Springs north. With such growth there may someday be a corridor of people all the way to Pueblo." They feel commissioned to cherish the thousands of people who are coming. "We've seen people whose lives are being changed by Christ who want to share their stories." He added, "As we keep growing, it is important that we grow in healthy ways. Health and growth go together. The Spirit is moving within these walls, but just building bigger institutions further out in the suburbs is not the point. Columbine taught us many things. The myth of moving out from the city to 'where the good schools are' was blown apart. So was the myth of suburban security and the myth of 'closure.' The answer is not just to be more cautious or to provide more security systems, nor even to provide a 'full service' church to keep people busy in a consumer society. Five years after the shootings we have 150 kids in confirmation, each one with a Lenten mentor. The place is packed on Wednesday nights for worship. Then we go off to talk about the faith. And as new people visit Christ, we do not simply say, 'How good to see you again,' but, 'I will be looking for you.' The Spirit continues to build and sustain community as we cherish and care for each other."

Back into the city

I stayed in Denver ten days during that visit and, as on previous visits, I stopped in at Our Saviors Lutheran near downtown. LaVonne, who according to some is the best cook in Colorado, was taking the scalloped potatoes and ham out of the oven. That, along with the green beans and pudding would feed 100 to 150 hungry people whom the congregation regularly nourishes at noon, sharing this ministry with other centers in the areas. I took a place beside Dorothy dishing up the dinner.

Edith, Hilda, and Margaret from Augustana Lutheran in the suburbs, part of a seniors group, had the kitchen under control. In the fellowship hall teenagers from a middle school were setting tables and greeting the guests. All was going well, when Jamie, about thirteen, came running into the kitchen, crying. "She's so nice. She's so nice." Jamie had been talking with a young, hungry, pregnant woman and discovered that she was friendly and loving, as well as needy. And she had a name: "Kim." This was Jamie's first direct encounter with a poor person. LaVonne comforted Jamie and assured her that tears were okay. "That's what happens when you begin to help people." She was a cook and a teacher of future workers of mercy.[5]

Later that day I walked the streets with members of the Urban Servant Corps, a faith community that provides opportunity for sustained service in the city.[6] The neighborhood is going through regentrification, so they are even more aware that for many a new, more affluent life in the city is still beyond reach. How does one really see the needs of people and cherish them, when the city tries so hard to hide its poverty? The pastor director asked, "Long after the national news media are gone, where is the spotlight and the public outpouring of grief when nine homeless people die?"

Questions for reflection and discussion

1.   During times of crisis how have you experienced people cherishing one another in deeply caring ways? How is this love extended in sustaining ways?

2.   How can we help each other see needs that the media may never notice, or not notice for long? How can we learn ways to be a Christlike presence in the world to change systems that trap people in violence, injustice, homelessness, poverty, . . . and wealth?

Bethlehem in Baldwin

Beautiful Baldwin, where people plant marigolds all over town, is five miles long and one mile wide on Long Island, New York. People moved out to this white, middle-class community from the city in large numbers after World War II. Baldwin became multiracial, multicultural, and interfaith in the 1970s. The pastor, quiet and caring, had insisted she come into Manhattan to meet me and we had taken the commuter train together out to the Island. We picked up her car at the station and drove to Bethlehem Lutheran Church. I noticed a sign in front announcing "Italian Night."

When the pastor was called to Bethlehem, she noticed the all-white worship leadership team and made a note to change that to a more diversified leadership. Soon an Iranian man, an architect, became a deacon. A man of West Indian heritage became an assisting minister soon after.

Bethlehem wants programs held in the church building to be an integral part of mission and outreach. They offer a Lutheran preschool four days a week, cherishing the one-and-one-half to four-year-old children. Weekly Bible studies become opportunities for outreach. The church council leads in mission. The process is simple: listen to the congregation members. What are their strengths? What are their growth areas? What dreams do they have for the future? Then they interview people from the community. What are the needs there?

Not that such a plan always goes smoothly. Struggles and internal conflicts are present in every congregation. But Bethlehem learned to not allow a few people to stand in the way of outreach. New York continues to be an immigrant city. People, including new immigrants, see this Lutheran church as a place where diverse people come together. The bishop told the congregation, "This is what the future of the Lutheran church looks like, right now." The pastor adds, "This is what the human family looks like, what the resurrected body of Christ looks like, and what people loving each other looks like." And "Italian Night"? She replied, "We have lots of Lutherans here with Italian heritage."

To be strengthened for continued mission, people need to see vision in action. For example, the congregation heard the message "We need to feed hungry people," but at council meetings, when wrestling with budgets, one would hear, "We can't afford . . ." So, the pastor put a jar in back of the church. Little by little it was filled. Finally there was enough money to offer one meal. Now they regularly serve over two hundred meals a month. They don't need the jar anymore; they have two freezers. In the midst of hesitance, even resistance, people want opportunities to act on their faith. Mission begins with cherishing people, which can lead to outreach, more people and more vision, and more connections and cherished relationships.

As we walked through the church building on this cold, mid-January Tuesday morning, I saw the preschool children. And I heard about the Pathfinders group, youth from kindergarten through seventh grade who come two Friday nights a month for dinner, worship, learning, and fun. Together they planned a living nativity. It is hard to find cows and sheep out on Long Island; somehow they came up with a llama. Pathfinders has grown into "Blessing Buddies" matching one adult with one child. A lonely, elderly woman was matched with a four-year-old. When she died the child wrote a note about her, which was put into the coffin. Through this cherished relationship the child learned that death is a part of life. The pastor said, "Because I was adopted, an only child, and my parents have both died, perhaps I am more aware of people feeling they don't belong. Inside of everyone there is an outsider." Bethlehem has small, caring shepherd groups for everyone in the congregation.

The pastor early in her ministry in Baldwin, became vitally involved in and then chair of the Interfaith Network that created ecumenical and interfaith study opportunities.[7] In developing a "school of religion," they engaged in "caring, sharing, and comparing" six weeks one spring. They used a panel discussion method that allows onlookers from the community, who are interested but not yet ready for discussion, to participate. At times almost one hundred people came to the meetings held at the Jewish temple from 8:45 to 9:45 in the evening. (These people are commuters.) "People are interested in religion and it's important they see religious leaders talking together," said the pastor "Where do we go from here?" is the next question.

I saw a pastor with quiet warmth and the skills of organization. She is carrying on strong, vital ministry cherishing, tending the people. Perhaps they could come up with only a llama, but I had seen a shepherd in the city.

A year and a half later: On another Tuesday morning: 9/11. I relived my journey on the commuter train out from Manhattan to Bethlehem. I called the pastor, and thereafter we talked regularly, almost daily at first. She said it helped to have someone outside to talk with, since everyone there was so personally, tragically, involved.

On September 11 itself the pastor contacted everyone she knew who might have a family member in lower Manhattan. The second day she called all the congregation's shut-ins because she knew they must feel isolated and afraid. On the third day she called the rest of the members because everyone's life was touched in some way. She talked with many children because they felt unsafe and insecure. One twelve-year-old girl had her bag packed. She wanted to leave New York.

On the evening of the third day, Bethlehem held a prayer service, open to the community. Bethlehem's former president, Kamy, from Iran, led the prayers. Bethlehem is his only family in this country, and although it was difficult, the congregation prayed together in the midst of their varied background and viewpoints. By the time of the Saturday evening neighborhood Bible study, congregation members were able to put their arms around Kamy and affirm his presence among them.

The second week was a week of despair; members reported racist rumors about Arab Americans in the community. Kamy, as an ambassador for Lutheran Immigration and Refugee Services said, "We have to be very careful that patriotism is not intermingled with hatred of immigrants." On Thursday night of the second week the community held an interfaith prayer service. Bethlehem's pastor, as chair of the Baldwin Interfaith Clergy Fellowship said, "That night one thousand people came. The fact that religious leaders here had a vibrant relationship before the crisis was so helpful."

Two and a half years later still: I talked with the pastor again. How does a congregation heal? Part of grief is anger. Some months after 9/11, conflict emerged in the congregation along old fault lines.

Those were difficult times. Growth dwindled. It was as though the congregation closed the shutters on its windows to the world for awhile. But now Bethlehem is once again opening up. The preschool is growing. The congregation is reaching out to new immigrants even more vigorously. Families from many different cultural backgrounds are becoming members. Vacation Bible school serves mostly families without a faith community. The pastor, who will soon be in her tenth year at Bethlehem, says she feels a renewed sense of call. "We are not defined by our fear, but by our faith."

In saying those words the pastor knew she was talking also about her own faith, because her husband's national guard unit had just been just been called up. He would be going to Iraq. "Our area, that lost so many people, is facing fear of loss again." The pastor described their two-and-one-half-year-old daughter, adopted from North Vietnam, who can't yet express in words what she is feeling, "So many children are suffering, here and in Iraq."

The pastor went on, "This country had a moment after 9/11 when the world was sympathetic. If we could have responded with nonviolence, we might have led the world. But rather we are experiencing how violence begets more violence. How can we find a way to love all human beings created in God's image?" What are the long-term effects of 9/11 on Bethlehem? "We value our relationships more deeply. We know we don't have all the time in the world. Our priorities are more keenly defined. Our deep anxiety continues, but our faith is deeper still. We have learned to cherish people . . . all people."

Questions for reflection and discussion

1. When towers (steeples) fall and grief abounds, in the midst of fear how can we cherish people of all faiths and nationalities?

2. How can small concrete act, like putting a jar in the back of the church, lead to broader mission? How can ecumenical and interfaith alliances increase and clarify vision for mission?

3. How does facing crises together both test and eventually strengthen a congregation? What crises has your congregation faced? Where are they now in opening or reopening their doors to the world?

Epilogue

After all of my travels, how would I conclude this book? There were so many stories yet to tell. I didn't want to stop. Literally on the final day of reading the page proofs, the ending rang in my ears right here at home. The bells of seven churches of Dubuque, Iowa, including our own, St. John's Lutheran, rang together for a full hour that Sunday evening.

Patrick Hazell, long time blues and jazz musician from Burlington, Iowa, had scouted out churches in close proximity with bells in their steeples for an hour-long concert. Dubuque's churches being downtown with the Mississippi River bluffs rising above was even better acoustically. Hazell had composed such concerts before, some in his hometown and the one in Izhevsk, Russia.

At 7:00 P.M. people gathered in the late summer daylight from all over Dubuque. They brought lawn chairs to sit in business parking lots, sat in their cars, or simply walked around to select a listening place. At this event, open to everyone, there was no "best seat in the house" for the privileged few. There was a man pushing a stroller, a woman in a wheelchair. Others heard from the bluffs above. People could listen while riding their bikes or walking the dog. Friends sat together with beer on the stoop or wine and cheese on the porch. The doors of St. John's were wide open. Members brought desserts and invited the neighborhood to come outside together.

I had assumed the composer would write music and ask bell ringers at each church to play their designated notes. But, no, the beautifully diverse sounds of the seven churches would make a much richer sound if each played their own distinct tone, diverse voices in ecumenical dialog. It began with one long, low bell. Then others joined. St. John's has three bells, still rung by hand. St. Luke's United Methodist has eleven, and First Congregational United Church of Christ has a single bell. A sister would push the switch to ring the bells at St. Raphael's Cathedral, the farthest away.

"Bells have overtones that don't show until played for a length of time. When multiple bells play, a synergy happens," said Hazell. "I give each bell a time to sound alone and in different combinations with the other bells. That gives the listeners a texture full of rhythmic and tonal interplay."

So it was with the churches in this book. Some churches do not have steeples or bells. But churches can find ways to open their doors and speak their voice outside in the public world. We can listen to the distinct voices of one another, not only ecumenically, but in interfaith dialog.

Just as congregations are called to reach out to all classes, cultures and races of people, the concert crossed demographics. Dubuque's commercial and residential growth is to the west. "This is a testament to the vitality of Dubuque's downtown, that it is still alive and its churches still active," said the pastor of St. John's. "I saw many people from the West end" he added. "Because the bells were ringing all around, the concert was mobile. People naturally encountered each other, intermingled, and shared the event."

Halfway through the concert, a man came out of the Italian restaurant two blocks from St. John's and started his power washer. A woman from the congregation ran over and asked if he could wait until 8:00. He did. Promptly at 8:00 she took him a dessert tray. A few minutes after 8:00 he started the washing. We usually don't ask each other to be so accommodating . . . nor thank one another when we are.

The music from the steeples continued. From the bluff one could see, beyond the steeples, cars on the freeway driving above the city traffic. With windows closed, places to go, did these people know church bells were ringing?

The conversation of the bells continued. For some, the steeple bells were merely backdrop to their busy lives. For many, the churches were a purposeful destination. They looked and really saw the crosses of the varied steeples. They also noticed that churches were not competing with one another.

Meanwhile, sounds of the city were not stilled. Dogs barked. A couple argued. Trucks passed. People came and went from a convenience store. A motorcycle assaulted the ears momentarily. The laughter of partygoers on the bluff rang out over the bells.

Slowly the sun's light dimmed. The bells rang on as the Creator turned the world. The composer had been inspired by the harmonic rhythms of insects chirping. One is reminded of the distinctive sound the leaves of various trees make blowing in the wind. Every night at twilight birds sing in our trees. Evensong.

And now, as 8:00 neared, night came. But the white steeple and gold cross of St John's did not grow dark. They seemed to glow more brightly, illuminated by the lights of the city. More and more bells chimed together. The sound rose and then, slowing, waned, ending again with one solitary bell. The party-goers paused and said, "Amen."

People went home. But many from these same communities of faith would meet outside again in two weeks for the annual CROP WALK to feed hungry people locally and around the world.

So many churches. All kinds of steeples. Open the doors! See all the people.

Notes

Chapter 1

1. H. Richard Niebuhr, *The Purpose of the Church and Its Ministry* (New York: Harper, 1956), 24.

2. The denomination reference is The Lutheran Church—Missouri Synod.

Chapter 2

1. Paul Minear, *Images of the Church in the New Testament* (Philadelphia: Westminster, 1960), 11-27. Minear says there are more than one hundred images if the Greek words are counted separately.

2. Matthew 27:46, 28:6-10.

3. See Hans Kung, *The Church* (New York: Sheed and Ward, 1967).

4. See the classic work by Avery Dulles, *Models of the Church* (Garden City, N.Y.: Doubleday, 1974). Dulles presents five models: the church as Institution, Herald, Sacrament, Communion, and Servant.

5. Norma Cook Everist, "Remembering the Body of Christ," *The Difficult but Indispensable Church,* ed. Norma Cook Everist (Minneapolis: Fortress, 2002), 45.

6. See that classic work by Jürgen Moltmann, *The Church in the Power of the Spirit* (New York: Harper and Row, 1975), 22, 64.

Chapter 3

1. In 1846 Dred Scott and his wife, Harriet, filed suit for their freedom in the St. Louis Circuit Court. This suit began an eleven-year legal fight that ended in the U.S. Supreme Court issuing a landmark decision declaring that Scott remain a slave.

2. "Tall Steeple" churches was a term used to describe churches that had or were expected to have a place of prominence in the community, a "prestigious" church, perhaps even a role of power and significance. Which denomination these churches belong to might vary with the area of the country, for example, Congregational in New England, Baptist or Methodist in the South.

3. Nathan Frambach, "Congregations in Mission: Rethinking the Metaphor of 'Family,'" *Currents in Theology and Mission,* Vol. 30 No. 3, ed. Norma Cook Everist (June 2003) 210-216. Frambach begins his article with the quote, "One of the most enduring features of the American landscape is the steeple, a landmark signaling the presence of a congregation" (210). He later warns, "The family metaphor is an appealing siren song that can lull a congregation into valuing privacy and intimacy above all else" (214).

Chapter 4

1. Sociologically, the church is a human community. See James Gustafson's classic work, *Treasure in Earthen Vessels* (New York: Harper, 1961). The church is a human, natural and political community; also a community of language, interpretation, memory and understanding, belief and action, and of social and theological interpretation.

2. The Wanamaker Grand Organ in Philadelphia has been thrilling shoppers each day since it first filled the Grand Court with music on June 22, 1911. Built for the 1904 St. Louis World's Fair, the original organ had 10,000 pipes. Today it has 28,500, the smallest ¼ inch, the longest 32 feet. It is now a National Historic Landmark.

3. See Joel Garreau, *Edge City: Life on the New Frontier* (New York: Doubleday, 1991). Garreau writes about entire new cities that are growing up in and beyond "bedroom" suburban communities with places of commerce and corporate enterprise.

4. Having served on many ELCA churchwide task forces, I realize that the Lutheran Center in Chicago in some ways physically resembles this office complex. However, I strongly disapprove of the negative caricature of "Higgins Road." Church bodies are incorporated and need office space just as congregations, I believe, need buildings. Real people with real lives serve inside these offices. My observations simply raise the questions of what such steeples and centers of meaning promise in and of themselves.

Chapter 5

1. Many factors shape the world outside our church doors, including the region of the country in which the congregation is located. Joel Garreau, *The Nine Nations of North America* (New York: Avon Books, 1981), xii. Traveling across the continent, Gareau presented a journalistic, sociological perspective of the nine distinctly different regions of North America. These have similarities to the nine regions of the Evangelical Lutheran Church in America, although the ELCA does not include Mexico and Canada.

2. Birmingham was not the only city with a negative image during the struggle for racial justice. Martin Luther King Jr. had written in mid-April 1963 from a Birmingham jail that time does not change things automatically. Martin Luther King, "Letter from Birmingham Jail," (Philadelphia: American Friends Service Committee, 1963), 9. People change racial images and realities.

3. Taken from 1 Thessalonians l:1-3. The greetings in many of the epistles are similar.

4. Now, a few years later, the area has a new Target and Dress Barn (on land where the homeless used to live). Shops provided for new, higher income people who bought up the last cheap land in Phoenix and are building homes in gated communities. Manny, a man from the neighborhood, commented, "They have to come out sometime!"

The money from the sale of Hope congregation's property went to a trust fund for urban ministry at Grace Lutheran, a few miles north, in an area of Phoenix some call "homeless central." The remnant of Hope was officially sent there. Grace has renamed their fellowship hall "Hope Hall" where they hold worship services and pancake feeds for the homeless. Money from the trust fund might be used again some day for a start-up church in south Phoenix. Hope's former building is used by the nearby Roman Catholic Church as a teen center.

5. Almost everywhere the passing of the peace was an occasion for me as a visitor to experience open hands and open hearts.

6. Look again at 1 Corinthians 12 as well as Romans 12 and Ephesians 4. "Now there are varieties of gifts, but the same Spirit; and varieties of services, but the same Lord; and there are varieties of activities, but the same God who activates all of them in everyone" (1 Corinthians 12:4).

Chapter 6

1. "McMansion" is a term that has been in use for the past decade or so. The word, formed from "McDonalds," the fast-food chain, plus "mansion" at first referred to cookie-cutter large new homes going up fast in this "dehumanizing, auto-dominated, market-research driven age." Sam Hall Kaplan, "Search for Environmental View of Design," *The Los Angeles Times,* July 17, 1990. Lately it has begun to refer to a large, opulent house, especially a new house that has size and style that doesn't fit in with the surrounding houses.

2. Luke 12:13-21. Jesus tells the parable of the rich man who produced abundantly who said, "And I will say to my soul, 'Soul, you have ample goods laid up for many years; relax, eat, drink, be merry'" (v. 19). But God said, "You fool! This very night your life is being demanded of you. And the things you have prepared, whose will they be?"(v. 20). Jesus warns, "So it is with those who store up treasures for themselves but are not rich toward God" (v. 21).

3. Norma Cook Everist and Nelvin Vos, *Connections: Faith and Life* (Minneapolis: Augsburg Fortress and Chicago: The Evangelical Lutheran Church in America, 1997). This four-unit, six-session each adult study uses an experiential method to connect basic tenets of the Lutheran faith with people's ministry in daily life.

4. Towns across the country, even in rural areas, are becoming bedroom communities. For example, Tipton Iowa, while not on a major highway, has people commuting in all directions: Iowa City, Cedar Rapids, the Quad Cities. Tipton has kept its attractive identity even though one-half of the population leaves town every morning.

Chapter 7

1. This author knows well the pervasive conflict pastors face that inflicts and weakens congregations. See Norma Cook Everist, *Church Conflict: From Contention to Collaboration* (Nashville: Abingdon, 2004).

2. I have seen congregations use a variety of creative ways to become accessible.

Wartburg Theological Seminary in Dubuque, Iowa, instead of adding a ramp in front of the chapel and refectory, actually raised the ground on the Quad, eliminating the formidable steps.

3. Note reference to this congregation at the end of chapter 5, in response to the question, "What if a congregation is being urged to close its doors?"

4. She quoted from Miroslav Volf, *Exclusion and Embrace: A Theological Exploration of Identity, Otherness, and Reconciliation* (Nashville: Abingdon, 1996). The pastor of Messiah asked the question, "How do we embrace each other? When things are broken we need forgiveness, but not forgiveness without justice." Reconciliation embraces our differences.

5. As this book goes to print, this nation marks the fiftieth anniversary of Brown v. Board of Education, the 1954 landmark U.S. Supreme Court decision against "separate but equal" in public education. The challenge of being a healthy pluralistic nation and of providing adequate funding for all school districts across economic dividing lines continue.

6. Jonah 4:9-11.

7. The group heard the entire Psalm 102. Verses 1 and 25 are quoted.

8. *Lutheran Book of Worship,* hymns 84 and 151. Years ago the congregation began by making the window over the front door, based on Psalm 121, "I lift my eyes to the hills. . . ." They are scheduled to finish the set with the Advent window.

Chapter 8

1. In John's gospel, the account of the disciples meeting together after Jesus's resurrection shows them behind locked doors (John 20:19). Jesus said to them two times, "Peace, be with you." One week later "although the doors were shut, Jesus came and stood among them and said, 'Peace be with you'" (John 20:26). Jesus's presence among us and the gift of the Holy Spirit (John 20:22) are absolutely necessary for us to unlock and open doors to serve in the world. Daniel Olson, professor of Pastoral Care at Wartburg Theological Seminary, Dubuque, Iowa, said that, "Lowering stress happens not simply when we rest or go on vacation, but when we engage in a challenge that is true to who we are and stretches us in that engagement in a way that gives meaning to our work" (May 10, 2004).

2. The story of the congregation she serves is told in chapter 1, "New Birth at Nativity."

3. Twelve students and one teacher were shot and killed by two other students, who then committed suicide, at Columbine High School, Littleton, Colorado, April 20, 1999. The fifteen deaths at Columbine has become a symbol for many more school shootings all over the United States in recent years.

4. See Ephesians 4: "The gifts he gave were that some would be apostles, some prophets, some evangelists, some pastors and teachers, to equip the saints for the work of ministry, for building up the body of Christ" (vv. 11-12).

5. While writing this paragraph, I received news of the death of Sister Marie Augusta Neal, whose work I have often quoted. I am compelled to note her work here in relation to Jamie's encounter with Kim. Marie Augusta Neal, *A*

Socio-Theology of Letting Go (New York: Paulist Press, 1977). Neal wrote of a "theology of relinquishment" in which the giver of aid does not offer help from a stance of domination, but rather "let's go" of power and resources that justice might be served. Neal, in addition to her teaching and impressive record of scholarly work, was known for her passion for social justice.

6. Many ELCA pastors and diaconal ministers serve in a wide variety of communities of faith, not in congregations.

7. See Kimberly Wilson, "Ordinary Friendship: The Ministry of Education," *Ordinary Ministry: Extraordinary Challenge,* Norma Cook Everist, ed., (Nashville: Abingdon, 2000), 167-171 for an account of educational ministry by this Lutheran pastor and a Jewish Rabbi.